HOW TO DEVELOP A POWERFUL AND POSITIVE PERSONALITY

Other books by Venkata Iyer

1. Systematic Reading Improvement (4 volumes), (1980)
2. Speaking Success (1981)
3. Excellence in Business Writing (1985)
4. Dynamic Reading Skills (1986)
5. Writing Readable Business Reports (1988)

How to Develop a Powerful and Positive Personality

VENKATA IYER

A Sterling Paperback

STERLING PAPERBACKS
An imprint of
Sterling Publishers (P) Ltd.
A-59, Okhla Industrial Area, Phase-II,
New Delhi-110020.
Tel: 26387070, 26386165; Fax: 91-11-26383788
E-mail: info@sterlingpublishers.com
www.sterlingpublishers.com

How to Develop a Powerful and Positive Personality
© 1998, Venkata Iyer
ISBN 81 207 2089 X
Reprint 2002, 2005, 2006, 2007

All rights are reserved. No part of this publication
may be reproduced, stored in a retrieval system or transmitted,
in any form or by any means, mechanical, photocopying,
recording or otherwise, without prior written permission
of the original publishers.

Published by Sterling Publishers (P) Ltd., New Delhi-110020.
Printed at Sterling Publishers Pvt. Ltd., New Delhi-110020.

PREFACE

Since 1968, I have been teaching this subject in some form or the other. Initially, the course used to be titled differently. Either because of the content or the teaching style adopted by me, it became more and more popular. Alongwith the increased popularity, I felt improvements were needed too.

Then it was Jayaram Shetty, the very able person who used to be in direct contact with people wanting to join the training programmes at the Indo-American Society, Mumbai, in January 1980, who casually suggested calling it Personality Development The title appealed to me for various reasons. And that is how the name was born to a training programme that became tremendously popular with the Indo-American Society, Mumbai.

Alongwith the name, the course, too, underwent further revision in its contents. Thus it has a teaching history since 1968. And, it is still going strong.

The Indo-American Society has supported me throughout the course. I am particularly grateful to Mr. Madhavan, Mr. Rajiv Vaishnav, Mr. Bhushan Desai, Mr. Karunakar Shetty, Mr. Jadhav, Mr. Kotian, Mr. Mama, Mr. Chotu and Mr. Jayaram Shetty, and all the others at the Indo-American Society, Mumbai. And very specially to Jayaram Shetty for suggesting the title and helping to make it more and more popular. The Indo-American Society, Mumbai, shall always hold a very special place in my life. I shall remain ever grateful to them.

Mr. Deepak Salve read the manuscript very carefully, with attention to every detail and suggested many valuable changes. I am truly grateful to him.

My relationship with S. K. Ghai of Sterling Publishers, New Delhi, is a special one. He is always ready to help. My books are being published with care, dedication and interest by his organisation. I shall ever remain grateful to S. K. Ghai and Sterling Publishers.

I dedicate this book to
Rajam, Ramesh, Geeta and Prabha.

Venkata Iyer

CONTENTS

Preface	v
1. The Choice is Entirely Yours	1
2. Principles of Personal Development	3
3. My Goals while Developing My Personality	6
4. Knowing the Self: The Key to a Better Quality of Life	8
5. The Basics	10
6. Personality	12
7. 24 Carats of a Winning Personality	20
8. Others Only Echo What We Whisper to Them in Silence	51
9. Art: An Aid in Understanding the World	56
10. Making Sense	61
11. Conviction Commands Commitment	65
12. Opportunity and Choice	69
13. Success	74
14. Self-image	81
15. Conditioning	86
16. Your Beliefs Affect Your Style of Functioning	92
17. Response Styles: Aggressive, Assertive, Passive	98
18. My Assertive Human Rights	104
19. Self-awareness Check: Response Style Assessment	111
20. Assumptions about People	114
21. Assertive Personality (Two Examples)	116
22. Developing an Assertive Personality	121

23. Acquiring an Assertive Personality: Where are You Now?	134
24. Motivation	137
25. Approaches to Mobilise the Motive Forces	142
26. Planned Personality Development	146
27. Skills Inventory	185
28. Attitudinal Changes	196
29. Knowledge: Means or an End?	201

1

The Choice is Entirely Yours

> "There is then a simple answer to the question, 'What is the purpose of our individual lives?'—they have whatever purpose we succeed in putting into them."
>
> A. J. AYER
> British philosopher

A popular African tale goes that once a certain man went through the forest looking for birds that he could add to his domestic possessions. He found a young eagle, brought it home and put it among his chicken and ducks. Even though it was an eagle—the king of birds—he fed it with mere chicken-feed and treated it just as any other member of his poultry farm.

Five years later, a naturalist happened to come to his house. When he went to see the poultry, he was shocked to find an eagle among the chickens, oblivious of its nature, strength and the opportunity for the freedom to be gained by the mere flapping of its wings. He pointed this out to the owner and said:

"That bird there, is an eagle. Not a chicken. How come you have that living among your chickens?"

"Yes, I know," said the owner. "But I have trained it to be a chicken. It is no longer an eagle. It is merely a chicken."

With his long study and observation to back him up, the naturalist could not accept this. He pointed out, "No. It can never be."

But the owner would not give up his point of view. So they agreed to test it. The naturalist picked up the eagle, held it high and spoke to it with great intensity: *"Eagle, Oh! King of the sky, you belong to the high heaven. You were born to fly high and not merely to exist in passivity in this cock-pen. Stretch forth your wings and fly. The sky is your abode. The sky is your limit."*

But the eagle remained confused, not knowing what was going on. He began looking around for support, and there he saw the chickens down below, quietly pecking on their feed, happy and contented. The eagle quickly jumped down and was once again comfortable and happy to be among the flock of his adoption.

The owner reminded the naturalist, "I told you it was a chicken."

"No," said the naturalist. "It is still an eagle. It has the heart of an eagle and I will make it soar high up to the heavens. Let us give it another chance tomorrow."

The next morning the naturalist woke up early and took the eagle outside the city, away from the houses, to the foot of the high mountain. The sun was rising, illuminating the top of the mountain with gold, and every creation was glittering in the joy of the morning glory.

He picked up the eagle and spoke to it in his most inspiring tone: *"Eagle, O! King of birds, you are an Eagle. You belong to the sky and not this earth. Your nature is to fly high. Your purpose is to rule. Your limit is the depth of the sky itself. Stretch forth your wings and fly."*

The eagle looked around and began to tremble as if a new life was coming to it. But, it did not fly. The naturalist then made it look straight into the shining, bright sun. Suddenly as if jolted by the shock, the eagle stretched forth its wings and with a screech, mounted higher and higher in the sky, never to return to the earth to remain contented to live like chickens.

It was an eagle, though it had been tamed and trained to remain as a mere chicken.

2

Principles of Personal Development

> "Life is a torment—on the other hand we can only face up to ourselves when we're afraid."
>
> THOMAS BERNHARD
> German poet

ALL DEVELOPMENT IS SELF-DEVELOPMENT

From the moment each one of us is born, the process of development begins. We did not know how to sit, how to coordinate the fingers, how to speak and to perform so many countless activities which we came to learn progressively and gradually.

There is also a definite need to develop yourself further as you voyage along through life. And a strong motivation towards accomplishing your goals is a must. It *must be* and *has been* generated within you too.

In many cases, the urge to consciously develop the self slows down. Sometimes it is even relegated to the back of awareness. The result is that most people stop growing in a true sense.

This will not do.

It is very essential that you realise that there is much to be learned and understood *about you, by you* and *for you*. It calls for efforts and a strong commitment to yourself. These must be self-motivated too.

No amount of coercion can produce growth and development in a person who is hostile, apathetic, or holds an I-do-not-care attitude.

DEVELOPMENT IS HIGHLY INDIVIDUAL

Many wise persons have used the term "Uniqueness of the individual".

Sometimes, when we ask people to introduce themselves to a group, many do come up with statements such as 'I am average,' whereas, in truth, each individual is *Unique*. How could *you* claim that you are average? What is the basis of your assessment? Or are you merely saying something for want of something better? Now, that is not fair. Because the views that you hold about yourself affects you in many ways, even if some of those things stated by you are said merely as a joke. *But, there are no human beings who are mere jokes. Are you a joke?*

It is also true that there is no average person. No two people have exactly the same needs. These needs differ from person to person. Now, all of this development and growth too are need-based. Because of this, human beings invent new products, new services and more novel and better ways of doing things. And, it is these human beings alone who can further development too.

There are many approaches to self-development. Different approaches work better with different individuals. These ways must be sought and implemented.

INDIVIDUAL DEVELOPMENT IS BASED ON DAY-TO-DAY EXPERIENCES

Experience is learning from what happens to an individual in day-to-day living.

Principles of Personal Development

Some people do claim that because they have become old, bald or senile, they are experienced but this is not necessarily true.

A new teacher was appointed in a school. In three years, he got promoted to a senior post superseding many others who had put in over 12 years work in the school. On being questioned about this impropriety, the school authorities gave a reply, *"You see, this person was here only for three years. But each year he learnt lessons from whatever was happening to him. Thus he has three years of valuable experiences. Honestly, how many new things and new ways did you learn through the years of your working here?"*

All of us must become aware of what is happening around us and determine what we want to accomplish in the short-term as well as in the long-term goals of our lives. This is a serious and purposeful aim.

EDUCATION IS CONTINUOUS

"Education," as Swami Vivekananda defined, *"is the process of manifesting the perfection that is already present within an individual."* In an age where education is being evaluated with the number of years spent in an institution and the number of degrees acquired, it would be appropriate to look at this definition in depth.

Education, truly, is not a process of pushing something into an individual. It is not the *collection of data within* that decides whether a person is educated or not. Conversely, the yardstick shall be how much he has *manifested, how much he has brought out from within, and how much he is applying to deciding on ways that are useful, productive and worthwhile.* Only these shall determine if a person is educated or not.

Thus, it is essential to ensure that a person must continue to strive for becoming wiser.

You and I have to make constant, consistent, and continuous efforts to improve the quality of our lives.

We must also seek as many methods as possible. And, we must feel very happy being so engaged too.

This is a continuous process. No one can claim that his education is complete and he has learned everything that there is to know. *Whatever you have done so far, to reach wherever you are, is not sufficient to keep you there.* This is the ultimate truth. If you stand still, you can only go backwards because the world around you is in continuous motion, going forward.

3

My Goals while Developing My Personality

> "Anyone who proposes to do good work must not expect people to roll stones out of his way, but must accept his lot calmly if they even roll a few more upon it."
> ALBERT SCHWEITZER
> German missionary

My purpose in working on my Personality Development is to ensure that:

I become more capable of *making INTELLIGENT CHOICES and find greater SELF-DIRECTION*. I lead my life. I take full charge of myself.

I become *WISER in my LEARNING and UNDERSTANDING*. I LEARN more to analyse and evaluate what is good for me. I learn more from my Day-to-Day EXPERIENCES.

My Goals while Developing My Personality

I continue to gain that *KNOWLEDGE which will help me to GROW and become HAPPIER.*

I become *more FLEXIBLE and INTELLIGENT in solving my PROBLEMS and find HAPPIER SOLUTIONS* that are acceptable to me, and if possible, to others too.

I experience *more FREEDOM and CREATIVITY within me.*

I become *more effective in gaining BETTER COOPERATION from others.* I realise that I do need people for leading a *HAPPIER life.*

I work, not merely for gaining approvals from others. *I do so in terms of MY OWN SOCIALISED PURPOSES.*

Note: This title, as well as the text, of this part is stated in first person singular. This is done to ensure that you can profit from the first reading, as well as from each effort.

4

Knowing the Self: The Key to a Better Quality of Life

> *"For him who sees this, who thinks this and who understands this, life springs from the Self. Hope springs from the Self. Fire, water, appearance, disappearance, food, power are known by the Self. So do the space, thought, will, speech, name, standing, meditation, sacred hymns, sacred rites, indeed all this world springs from the Self."*
> CHANDOGYA UPANISHAD

Next time you go to a circus show, take a closer look at those powerful elephants standing calmly outside the tents. They are tied to wooden poles with flimsy looking ropes. These elephants seem happy, meek and contented, oblivious of the tremendous strength they possess.

I have often asked, "Why can't they pull off those poles and be free? Why do they remain there like some puny little 'Yes Men'?"

Looking at what is happening now, we may not find the answer. The present for many, as in this example, is only a cold statement of what happened in the past. But, the future will be based on what is done now.

When the elephant was young, it was caught, and tied to a steel pillar or a huge tree with steel chains. Every time it had pulled hard on the chain, it only got hurt.

In a few weeks, the trainers succeeded in making the animal believe that there was no use trying.

The elephant has stopped searching for its freedom.

Like that elephant, many human beings too have stopped searching for more free, self-dependent ways that shall contribute to a better quality of life and living.

The key to that *better quality* is to be found within. It has to be searched systematically. And, it can be done. And, it can be found.

5

The Basics

> *"The important thing in science is not so much to obtain new facts as to discover new ways of thinking about them."*
> SIR WILLIAM BRAGG
> British scientist

A FUNCTIONAL DEFINITION

Reference books define *Personality* as *"The integrated organization of all the Psychological, Intellectual, Emotional and Physical characteristics, especially as they are presented to others."* That means the sum total of everything that a person is.

DEVELOPMENT

Personality Development is an ongoing process; always partial, flowing and progressive. No personality is ever fully DEVELOPED or UNDEVELOPED. Personality development starts from the time of birth. Efforts made through proper awareness can make that development Productive, Useful and Worthwhile.

The Basics

And, whatever we have done so far to reach wherever we are, is not sufficient to keep us there.

A KEY TO PERSONAL SUCCESS

In the pursuit of Personal Success, nothing else is more important than *the development of a Winning Personality*.

Within the context of this book, we are essentially concerned about this goal.

Developing a Winning Personality is not a hit-and-miss affair nor is it a matter of mere luck. Society's values keep changing. Norms get outdated. Thus, the competence and personal attributes that are needed to remain as a useful, productive and happy member of the society too need updating.

Even an alert and informed individual must occasionally wonder whether he or she is flexible enough to survive. If we do, and when we do this, we shall move closer towards our Goals of Fulfilment, Happiness and Success.

THE NON-VERBAL FACTOR

"What you are," said Ralph Waldo Emerson, *"speaks so loudly, I cannot hear what you say."*

All of us interact with others all the time. We do it by the use of words, actions, facial expressions, tone of voice, gestures and even silence. And each contributes in some way to the understanding. However, if there is a conflict between what was said and what was felt, we shall tend to believe what was felt by us and not what was told to us.

Someone tells me that he is honest and truthful. But his behaviour makes me feel that he is neither honest nor truthful. What shall I believe? His words or his behaviour?

We often listen to the personality of the other person rather than merely to his words. We see, feel and then listen.

6

Personality

> While moving through the desert on horseback, the son of a cowboy asks, 'Dad what does a rattlesnake look like?'
> The answer was, 'My son I don't have to tell you. When you see one, you will know instantly.'

The word Personality comes from its Latin origin, 'Persona'. It meant the mask an actor wore to suit the role he was playing. In a sense, each of us plays many roles in our lives. Sometimes, the role is that of a parent. Next, it may be of a husband. Then it could be of a son or a daughter, an employee, a student, a colleague and so on. All these roles must be played well.

Every role calls for a different projection of the personality. And, this is said in a very healthy, positive sense.

To those who are close to me, my personality shall often indicate my emotions. I rarely have to use words to tell them whether I am joyful, caring, angry or sad.

But what about the many others with whom I have to interact everyday? Thus, it is essential for us to know those personality factors that are relevant while interacting with others.

Personality

In an article published by the *Readers Digest* titled, 'Can You Read Body Talk?' it was said that words play only a limited role in creating an impact in any face-to-face interactions. They had also mentioned that there are three components.

American psychologist, Albert Mehrabian in 1967, had even listed the relative importance of these three factors after considerable research:

Physical Factors	55%
Vocal Factors	38%
Verbal Factors	7%

In another report*, Dr. Ray Birdwhistell, Professor of Anthropology, University of Pennsylvania, had concluded:

In a situation in which someone must make a decision and is receiving contradictory messages—a job interview, a sales presentation, a proposal to the superior etc.—the understanding arrived is based:

7% on the literal meanings of the words said,
38% on the way the words are said (tone, timbre, accent, speech rhythm, phrasing, loudness, conviction, etc.) and,
55% on messages that have nothing to do with words at all.

This last 55 per cent include the personality reactions, the appearance, the clothes worn, briefcase carried, the style of haircut, glasses worn, how the hand was shaken, where and how we sat in the waiting room, how early or how late we were, status symbols like a car, the fountain-pen, or even the number of seconds it took the visitor to pass from the outer office to the desk of the person he had come to meet.

You may not want to believe in these numbers and their relative importance. But it cannot be denied that the Personality factors are of paramount importance in any interaction.

And, there is nothing new in these research findings too. Even the primitive man knew about these. In fact, his major means of communication was through personality and to some extent through the voice. In those days, there was no language as we know it today.

Take any performing art. Take drama. Take dance.

Body Language—Clue or Crock, Richard H. Tyres, Training Management, Motivation and Incentives, Winter 1979.

In India, we have many ancient art forms like Bharatanatyam and Kathakali. The major components that communicate are the personality of the artist and the non-verbal factors. (The term 'verbal' means those factors relating to words. 'Non-verbal' means all those factors that are beyond the words.)

The next time you watch any performance, be it a very formal one, or a very informal one like any day-to-day happenings, check this. You will know what this means.

Many do not have an awareness of this vital aspect of personality. Is it possible to enforce a rule such as *"Do not watch me. Do not feel me. But, merely accept my words as final"*?

In developing our personalities further, it would be wise for us to consider some of the factors that can help us to project it more positively.

1. BE LIVELY

Show signs of life. Every great performer will tell you about the extreme importance of remaining fresh, lively and alert during a performance.

There can be nothing more demoralising than to be forced to go along with someone who is dead-tired, dejected, and demoralised.

Dame Nellie Melba, the Australian soprano, was often referred to as the 'Goddess of Opera'. First trained to be a pianist, she slowly rose to international glory and achieved the pinnacle of success as a singer with a high and flexible coloratura voice. She was made the Dame of the British Empire in 1918.

While talking about her personal discipline and habits, she once mentioned that any main meal she took had to be at least three hours prior to the performance. In the intervening time, she would also rest and relax as much as possible. She needed all her energy to perform her art.

After the performance, which could last two to three hours, happy but famished, she would consume a hearty, heavy meal. To finish it off, she was also fond of devouring a few pieces of peaches topped up with a load of vanilla ice-cream. This dessert itself has come to be called as 'Peach Melba', named after this famous personality.

Dame Melba knew the significance of putting all her energy into every performance. The next time you tend to be a little

Personality

careless before an important discussion, remind yourself of Peach Melba.

Whenever you interact with people, and you do want to succeed too, *be lively*.

2. BE ENTHUSIASTIC

Enthusiasm is defined as a strong excitement or feeling on behalf of a cause, something that inspires or is pursued with ardent fervour.

You will be enthusiastic when you believe that you are engaged in a worthwhile, useful and productive job, and you are going to enjoy it. Such a belief will alter your body chemistry. You will begin to enjoy whatever you may be doing. Others will perceive it too, because enthusiasm is contagious.

Haven't you noticed this? Say, when you were feeling dejected, someone else came and altered your mental state quickly. The other person's enthusiasm rubbed off on you and your mood changed.

In the sales profession the saying goes, "The salesman who is not fired with enthusiasm, *must be fired with ENTHUSIASM.*"

3. BE PROPERLY ATTIRED

Whenever you were dressed neat and smart, you did feel neat and smart. Now, try to act neat and smart when you know your attire itself is not so. Try.

The manner in which we appear to be, has a direct effect on us as well as on others. And these things do affect the way our personalities get projected too.

When in public, decorum demands that we appear in a certain acceptable manner.

Perhaps you feel very comfortable in casual or fancy clothes. But, can you wear them when you have to conduct a seminar for senior managers? You must conform to ethics and expectations. When you do, you shall be projecting your personality to your advantage. Remember, the key components here are 'ethics' and 'expectations'.

Why do most offices insist that their employees wear neat, smart and acceptable clothing while in their workplace?

Maybe it is true that you have every right to appear in whatever form you may like. But if your attire should affect the other persons adversely, you may create a wrong impression.

Maybe you feel that this factor is not very important. Perhaps, this is so. But being groomed well, you stand to gain. So, why not?

4. WEAR A PLEASANT OUTLOOK

A Chinese saying goes, "A man without a smile, must not open a shop."

A smile reflects an inner glow. The smile melts the fears and arouses favourable responses. When done with a certain degree of genuine concern for another's feeling, it says, "I like you. I am concerned about you. Treat me as your friend."

Many successful organisations know the need for this. They spend huge sums of money to keep their premises clean and attractive. They adorn their walls with expensive paintings. They maintain mown lawns. These things make those who work there as well as those who visit, feel good. The company is smiling at them.

A smile reflects an inner joy. Apart from this, if we can believe those expert researchers, a smile is good for your health too. It is often quoted that it takes 56 muscles to frown, while it takes only 16 muscles to smile. Why tire your muscles through frowning?

Be pleasant. It is good common sense to be so.

5. ELICIT CONFIDENCE

Confidence is a matter of successful experiences. Failures do not produce confidence. The athlete running the hurdles will find the first one difficult, the second less difficult and the third, lesser still. Because of the successes behind him, he knows he can do it.

When a person is confident, he is saying '*I can*'. The difference in the opposite case is only a 't', between "I can" and "I can't".

The famous quote attributed to William James is relevant to us here:

> *Actions seem to follow feeling, but action and feeling go together. But, by controlling our actions, we can indirectly control our feelings.*

Even on a hot summer afternoon, you can see salesmen moving about with a smile, wearing smart clothes with ties included. They have learned to control their actions, and they have been able to control their feelings too.

Even when you are emotionally upset, if a guest should walk into your house, you will put up a cheerful appearance and welcome the guest. You are controlling your actions. The feelings are sure to follow.

Patients expect the surgeon to be confident. Listeners expect the speaker to be confident.

Why appear negative, when you can project yourself positively? Acting confident is easy. Anyone can do it. You too.

6. REMAIN POISED

A well-balanced, calm and collected personality generates acceptance and respect from others. More so, when there is an amount of hostility or cause for unfriendliness.

In my childhood, I have often thought about an incident which my father would narrate. A cruel British officer, during the days of India's struggle for Independence, was well known for the most inhuman treatment he would mete out to Indians. He had once gone to arrest Mahatma Gandhi and was ready to beat him up. But, face to face with the great leader, all the hostility of the officer dissolved, and he could not gather enough courage to be cruel to Gandhiji.

I have spent many nights thinking about *how* and *why* such a thing could happen. The answer, I believe, lies in that quality of *equanimity* or *equipoise* or simply *poise*.

Children will chase only those dogs which agree to be chased by them. Not the ones who face them.

When a new teacher walks into the classroom, the initial behaviour of the students shall be based on the 'poise' of the teacher conveyed to them.

Probably, this ability to remain unruffled even in the face of adversity, is the singlemost important quality of a winning personality.

In our spiritual texts, they refer to a lotus leaf in water. Although it is fully immersed in water, it never gets wet. The leaf stays above the water and remains dry too.

If you ever have to face hostility, you have to remain poised. Your personality will guide you to find the way out.

7. LOOK INTO THE EYES

Any interaction between people is a two-way process. Mere words, no matter how accurate or well chosen they are, do not take us far. The other person must perceive the intended meanings. For this purpose, a feedback is essential.

If we have to reach others, maintaining contact through the eyes becomes most essential.

Swami Ramdas is a well-known sage from India. While referring to those days of wandering in the wilderness, he speaks about the use of eye contact and poise. When face to face with a wild animal, he advises us to look deeply into the eyes of the animal with full courage and poise. Soon, he assures us, the animal will quietly walk away.

By this eye contact, he tells us that the animal will understand that you have no intentions to cause any hurt, nor are you planning to run away.

Leaders who have faced hostile or unfriendly crowds, but have also won them over, tell us about the need to maintain poise and eye contact.

To shy away could mean an attack from the other end.

Eye contact does not mean 'aggression'. Nor does it mean 'attack'. It means self-control and the courage to face the situation.

	All the time					*Never*
1. Whenever I interact with people, do I remain lively and full of energy?	5	4	3	2	1	0
2. Whenever I am engaged in working with myself and with others, am I enthusiastic about myself?	5	4	3	2	1	0
3. Whenever I appear before others do I take care to ensure that I am dressed in neat, clean and acceptable clothes?	5	4	3	2	1	0
4. Am I generally pleasant and smiling whenever I interact with others?	5	4	3	2	1	0
5. Do I elicit certain confidence whenever I interact with others?	5	4	3	2	1	0
6. Do I maintain poise while I am engaged in interacting with others?	5	4	3	2	1	0
7. Do I make sure that I look into the eyes of others during my interactions?	5	4	3	2	1	0

My total score on Personality Projection: _____ out of 35

CONCLUSION

These seven components are the basics when it comes to learning about Personality Projection. Think deeply about these and start practising them. You will begin to enjoy the results.

Now, how would you rate yourself on each of these components? Circle the number in the range that most closely describes how you see yourself in relation to each of these.

7

24 Carats of a Winning Personality

> "The first men who were contemporaries of Cronus enjoyed complete happiness. It was the GOLDEN AGE.
>
> "Hessoid says: 'They lived like gods, free from worry and fatigue; old age did not afflict them; they rejoiced in continual festivity. Their lot did not include immortality, but at least, they died as though overcome by sweet slumber. All the blessings of the world were theirs; the fruitful earth gave forth its treasures unbidden. At their death, men of the Golden Age became benevolent genii, protectors and tutelary of the living.'"
>
> THE ORIGINS OF HUMANITY
> Greek mythology

A winner, like gold, is 24 carats fine.

Gold, is a malleable, ductile, yellow, metallic element.

It is trivalent, meaning a valence three (relative capacity to UNITE, REACT, and INTERACT), and univalent (chemical valence of one).

Very ductile and most malleable of metals, flexibility is its most amazing characteristic.

A relatively soft metal, it is hardened by alloying with other metals and yet it will continue to project its own individuality.

Gold is widely distributed on this earth. It is also found in various forms of dust, grains, flakes and even nuggets.

It is highly valued as wealth and many magical properties are attributed to it.

Gold is generally accepted as a means of balancing international accounts.

A winner is all these and much more.

According to Muriel James and Dorothy Jongeward, celebrated authors of *Born to Win*:

> *A WINNER is one who responds authentically by being Credible, Trustworthy, Responsive and Genuine; both as an individual and as a member of the society.*

"*All that glitters, is not gold*" goes the old adage. In this modern age (Iron Age as the Greek might term it), Man has found many substitutes for this precious metal. Some of them even glitter more. But they are not 'Gold' to us.

A WINNER is genuine. Although trivalent, he/she continues to be univalent too. Success, or life, to them is not a destination, but a flowing changing journey in which nothing is fixed.

Being unique, something new, something never created or existed before, winners have special ways of seeing, hearing,

---

Note: Wherever we shall use the term *WINNER* in this book, it shall be done in the wider context mentioned earlier.

In the following pages, these 24 carat counts are explained in detail. After studying each count, and understanding it well, you will be required to score yourself on a scale of 0 to 5 for each of the count. The question before you is to make an assessment of how many points you would give yourself *today* for each of the count.

You are not to spend too much time calculating the number of points you deserve. You must also not put off that decision for another day. Do it immediately on reading each item. You will of course have opportunities to review each at a later date.

For now, assess yourself straightaway. No one else need to know your scores because it is your own assessment of yourself.

smelling, touching, tasting and thinking as no one else can. There are no fixed classifications about them. Rich or poor, male or female, tall or short, young or old, black, brown or white, winners are everywhere.

You might be tempted to argue that the winner is a myth, a fictional character, a fantasy or a mythological hero. But as you *assay* each of the *'carat-erstics'*, you too will discover that the winning personality is real.

CARAT COUNT NO. 1

Distinct, Distinguishable and Definite

How deeply have you thought about yourself? Do you have an answer to the question, 'Who am I?'; an answer which *you* are fully satisfied with? Take a closer look at those answers you do come up with.

Have you ever considered that you are not an ordinary, mass-produced, mass-conditioned-to-conformity, indistinguishable-from-the-crowd human being?

You are not just about anybody. You have very specific traits and qualities that are definite only for you.

You have your own special ways of thinking, working, moving, eating, loving, living and doing so many other things.

Are you just about an ordinary, average person? Can you show me an average person?

You are a distinct, distinguishable and definite individual. I too am.

When we permit ourselves to think that winning is something, that has only to do with something outside us, and only then, we lose this quality of individuality. The day that specific quality is lost, you are as good as dead.

The world will be only too happy to turn anyone into a pendulum. Have you ever noticed that the pendulum has no power of its own to move? Nor can it come to a stop by itself? It is always wound and pushed by the whims and fancies of someone else.

Each human being has distinct, distinguishable and definite personal qualities. Each one must know these clearly and use them for their own advantage.

Not a single person upon this earth fits neatly into any roles, job designations, community patterns, academic qualifications, financial strata, religion, language, colour or sex. They are in them and, yet, are beyond them.

To them :

> *Style is no substitute for substance.*
> *Knowing certain facts is not more powerful than simple wisdom.*
> *Creating an impression is not more potent than being oneself.*

The person who is down-to-earth can do what needs doing more effectively than that person who is merely busy.

Look for the winner in your own personality.

My Score	0	1	2	3	4	5

CARAT COUNT NO. 2

Capacity to Enjoy, to Laugh

The capacity to enjoy life, to laugh, is a very special gift granted to each of us. Laughter is a very unique gift and only human beings are endowed with it. Can animals laugh the way we can? To the best of my understanding, this laughter is possible only by human beings.

Do you laugh sufficiently? We are not talking about laughing at the expense of others. But just laugh. To enjoy oneself. To relax. As a sign of being alive. Because you see so many wonderful things around you. Because you see and experience joy within you as well as around you.

Winners are comfortable with everything in life. They enjoy life.

They see so many wonderful colours even in the rain-filled clouds of life.

Meet them on the streets and enquire: "How are you?" The spontaneous answer will be, "Wonderful! Couldn't have been any better."

They enjoy just about everything in life. Trees, animals, movies, picnics, sports, soap-bubbles, day-to-day work, emergencies, cities, villages, travelling, mountain climbing, swimming, watching birds fly in formation, and singing in the rain or in the bathroom. They have no time for grumbling, fault-finding, back-biting or the world-is-about-to-crumble facial expressions. They are busy thriving.

If it is dry, well, that's it.
If it is humid, it's still another beautiful day.
If it is raining, it's great fun to watch the raindrops fall and sing in the rain.
If it is cold, how nice it is to wear warm clothes and swing around.

Do you often consider how wonderful it is to be alive? Have you developed the capacity to see those many beautiful things that are happening around you? Do you feel the freshness and joy that every new day brings to you? Do you relate to everything in life with your capacity to enjoy life, to relish it, and to laugh?

Are you busy adding life to the years that you are living in?

My Score	0	1	2	3	4	5

CARAT COUNT NO. 3

Freedom from Excuses and Guilt

Right from the moment I became conscious about myself, I have been made to offer excuses about why I did a certain thing the way I did. Someone else did not like what I did. It did not suit his or her convenience or expectations. So, I was made to offer an excuse for my being what I was. No one was interested in my 'truth'.

When I got the first progress report from my school authorities, I felt very happy. Someone gave a progress report to me too. And, it was a wonderful feeling to carry it to my parents. But, the school teacher felt that I had failed in two topics.

But, when they (my parents) looked at the report, they started screaming, weeping and even beating me. Why? Because, according to them, I was a failure. "How can their son ever become anything worthwhile in his life?" This is what they were overly concerned about.

Why? Just because I did not score sufficient marks in some silly topics. The result was, I had to find excuses. And, in due course, I found many of them. "The teacher did not teach well." "Others too failed." "Questions were tough." When I began to offer those excuses, my parents were happy, even though they still punished me. So I had to find more convincing excuses. I developed and learned all kinds of excuses for all occasions. (Eliminating most of them also took many years.)

Do you need any excuses for whatever you genuinely are?

You won't find a winner say, "If only I had joined the Engineering College," or "I agree with what you say, but what to do? My parents were not very rich and that's why I am..."

Winners realise that *Excuses are worse than lies. They are lies guarded.*

Winners shall not waste their time thinking and expressing that things were not what they really were. Instead, they are busy planning, working, learning and improving. They accept themselves without finding any excuses to do so.

Feeling guilty about what happened in the past is strictly prohibited for them. The only reality is the present. The now, stillness, clarity, and consciousness are more immediate than any number of expeditions made into the distant lands of one's mind.

They have no time make others feel guilty too. You will hear them say, "Oh! Forget about it. You don't have to say sorry to me." "Let's talk about what is to be done now." They are so clear about their self-respect that many of the cheap tricks based on guilt-manipulations will not cut ice with them. Winners have no time to feel guilty nor see others feel miserable due to guilt. They have buried their 'ifs' and 'buts', and, with them, all the excuses that prevent them from growing up.

My Score	0	1	2	3	4	5

CARAT COUNT NO. 4

Freedom from Anxiety, Tensions and Worry

How do you react to situations that are inherent with tensions and anxiety? Do these generally drain you of much peace, serenity and creative energy? Have you ever quietly thought what these are, and how you should face them?

Let us take *worry*. It is a common, natural, negative internal reaction. It starts with an essential need to perform some definite actions. It has a concern behind it, "Oh my God, what will happen now?" There is some definite cause behind such a concern. And, it is natural too. That concern originated from the need to perform some definite action. When the needed action is *not* performed, and instead, the person allows himself to remain in a state of negative concern, the worry becomes destructive and shatters the mental state.

Winners shall accept that concern as natural. They shall start thinking, "What should I do now? What precautions and actions should I take to look after my interests?" When we start adopting such a let-us-face-it approach, the energy gets directed towards finding practical solutions. We begin performing the required action. Now all the energy goes into a positive direction. The individual becomes creative.

Thus, when you understand this, you shall become busy living the present moment creatively. You start developing so many goals to pursue *now*, and become busy with them. Where is the time to worry and fret about things that cannot be controlled without action carried out now? Winners refuse to accept worry as a substitute for living in the present.

They make choices leading to results. They do not worry or waste time merely thinking about consequences.

Anxiety is a natural concern for the outcome. It is perfectly normal. And, there is nothing wrong with it too. Winners accept them and get busy with those actions to be performed *now*. With such an attitude, the anxiety is turned into a powerful, supportive, creative force within. In a positive sense, anxiety is useful and essential.

The beginning of any anxiety should be taken as a signal for something that is needed to be done. *"What is to be done now?"* Winners *do* react that way.

Tension is an essential part of life. It is necessary for the body too. You cannot even hold your hand straight if sufficient tension does not exist in those muscles. Thus, the problem begins when you do not understand what tension is, and thus, add more unwanted tensions. Winners shall accept the fact that a certain amount of tension is essential to achieve any goals, and, in the process, the problem gets solved.

All winners seem to have developed a triggering-off system which ensures that the present moment is not wasted in future anxiety, tensions or worry.

My Score	0	1	2	3	4	5

CARAT COUNT NO. 5

Living Only in the Present, Here and Now

Observe anyone who is creative. Take a farmer. Take an engineer or an artist. Take your mother or your spouse. Think of yourself as an example. Every achievement you have ever made has come through actions performed in the present; here and now.

Yesterday has gone forever. It is a cancelled cheque.
Tomorrow doesn't exist. When tomorrow shall come, it shall be today. Tomorrow is only a promissory note.
Today is real. It is ready cash.

Winners understand this truth. They are pragmatic, genuine individuals. They observe life deeply and learn from everything that is happening to them now.

They are people who plant the seeds now that shall bear fruits in the future. They understand and practise this law of nature.

To winners, moments between every activity is as true as the activities themselves. They are not postponers, and, the future holds no threat to them. They remain busy now.

The society might choose to brand them as careless people because they do not conform to others' wishes. But they go about their jobs irrespective of what other people may say, think or do.

They are careful. Yes, they are. But, they are certainly not busy counting their pennies, dreaming of the future and remaining content with living in abject misery today.

They have seen fruit trees grow. The farmer selects the seeds, prepares the earth, plants those seeds, waters them, nurtures them, takes care of them for long, and watches them grow into healthy trees. And in return, a single seed that was planted and nurtured by him blossoms into a thousand fruits by the blessings of nature.

Did you ever meet a tomorrow face to face? Can you bring back a yesterday to your present day? They are mere hopes and memories. They can only serve as goals and lessons for all you shall do with your today.

Winners believe in the concept *"Life is all action now."*

Live now. Be active now. Make every moment into a moment of fulfilment.

My Score	0	1	2	3	4	5

CARAT COUNT NO. 6

Self-reliant, Self-dependent Relationships

To succeed in life, all of us need to become *strikingly independent*. Relations and relationships to us *should not* be built on dependence. We need to develop that uncanny knack of remaining free, independent, and yet cultivate healthy relationships with people.

Freedom of thinking, freedom of deciding and freedom of acting in terms of our own values is a must if you and I have to accomplish anything that is productive, worthwhile and useful in life. To live happily in this world, a relationship too is a need and a must. It is a reality of life. Because of this purpose, a relationship has to be built on fulfilling mutual needs. It has to be caring, supportive and worth cherishing. It can never be allowed to become a bondage.

The *winners* that we are learning about *do love people*. They do. They have very strong emotional ties with their family members and friends. But, if a member of their social unit should make unreasonable demands on their time and efforts, they can courageously and yet affectionately decline those overtures. If the other person chose to suffer unhappiness which was not of *my* making, then it is not *my* problem. It is *his* or *her* problem. "I do want to help them. But first they must realise that they have a problem on their hands. Only then can I help them." This is a winner's conviction.

To be successful and happy, you and I have to be lovable. But we cannot afford to get involved in numerous relationships too. We need to be selective and sincere, genuine and sensitive about our love.

A relationship is not automatically brought about through advantages of birth. It has to be created, cultivated and maintained through understanding, respect and mutual affection, irrespective of caste, creed, colour or position in the society.

To be a winner, we need to become a model of caring, nurturing adults, with abundant love at every stage, always encouraging and demanding self-reliance, self-dependence and self-assertion.

My Score	0	1	2	3	4	5

CARAT COUNT NO. 7

Freedom from Approval-seeking

Bertrand Russell in his book, *The Conquest of Happiness*, tells us that *sinning is when we continue doing those things which incur our own disapproval.*

Winners are not sinners.

Simple common sense tells us that if we do not approve anything ourselves, we must not do it. Therefore, whatever we have to perform as a part of our legitimate existence, we cannot afford to disapprove ourselves. But others will always find ways to locate faults in my actions. This is a way of the world. If everything I do has to be approved by others, how can I exist?

Winners approve of their own actions. They do. They listen to their inner voices very closely. Because they hear the approval emanating from within, they are not busy seeking approval from outside.

I have been approached by certain people saying that if I am willing to donate a certain amount of money to a specific organisation, they shall award a medal to me citing me as an outstanding citizen. If I accept such an offer, and do acquire one and exhibit such a medal, others may approve visibly. But what about my own self? I know I bought it. I could have even bought one myself from the market or got such a medal made myself. It would possibly have been cheaper too.

There is no need to suit our actions to seek honour and recognition. The ideal path is to deserve it. Honour shall come to us because we deserve it.

The award in the final analysis has to come from within.

Winners usually remain free from moulding their actions based simply on what other people may think, say or do. They have no time for cheap manipulations of others to suit their own convenience.

Being human, it is only natural that each of us like recognition and awards. But, we have to deserve it first. *An approval received without the approval of the self, is no approval; but a deception. Self-deception.* You and I can never stoop to such levels. Conversely, buying an award after knowing why I am doing it, and if I approve of my action too, then maybe there is nothing wrong with it too. But, I would rather deserve it first.

Putting on a mere show, behaving as if you are something which you are not, and doing so merely for seeking approval, is a waste of creative energy.

My Score	0	1	2	3	4	5

CARAT COUNT NO. 8

Clarity on Social Values

You and I are not rebels out to change and destroy the old order. We are an integral part of the social system. But, we certainly want to make improvements that are worthwhile, useful and productive.

This society is engaged in performing so many rituals, merely because others have been doing so. Possibly, many of them could have been started with a valid cause and intentions too. But many of them are outmoded and irrelevant to current needs.

Others may be attending and throwing elaborate parties even when they can ill-afford it. Why? Because others are doing it. Because it is a convention that must be followed. Deep within, they also know that there is much that is irrelevant, meaningless and outdated. To the winner, all these need not be aped blindly. They need not follow them because others too are engaged in doing them.

For instance, birthday parties of a child are not occasions for the parents to have a great time while the child is ignored or imprisoned with a caretaker in a remote corner of the house.

A winner neither contributes to nor participates in the 'corruption' that has become an integral part of public life today. *How can I accept a bribe for performing some legitimate work for which I am already paid by my employer?*

A winner shall develop such well-defined, relevant social values that have meaning and purpose. He shall adhere to them, practise them and live by them. If he does not follow some short-sighted, long-lost, over-used, outworn social customs, in due course people shall start respecting him. And (again in due course), shall follow him too. Thus, he succeeds not only in changing those social values that were irrelevant, but also leads by example. Thus, the winner shall live better within the society which shall approve of him too.

Initially, the society might choose to call these people rebels. The winners do realise this possibility and accept it too.

They understand and accept the society as an important part of their lives. But they also realise that a society will respect an individual only when he stands by his convictions, irrespective of outside pressures that could be coming from various motives.

Winners hold respect for every person and every relevant issue. They do not dismiss any encounter as insignificant. Neither do they become anxious nor afraid of being overwhelmed or embarrassed. They have thought about their social value systems, and are clear about them too.

My Score	0	1	2	3	4	5

CARAT COUNT NO. 9

Laughing and Spreading Joy
Is it not true that you can recall certain people straightaway as someone you would love to have as company in a party? Is it because they can crack wonderful jokes? Or is it because they can pull down someone (who is not present in the party) so cleverly? Or is it because they are so good at ridiculing the opposite sex, particularly in strictly unisex parties?

I think the true answer lies in something else. Those personalities are so good at knowing how to laugh, and in the process create joy and laughter among others too.

You could have heard their laughter even in a crowd. Often theirs was the only one in that crowd. Something touched a funny bone and the laughter came flowing spontaneously. They did not bother about the timing, the decorum or about the presence of so-called dignitaries positioned on a high pedestal.

There are so many performers in the arts world that you look forward to meeting them. Their mere appearance and presence make you feel happy. Their personalities are so developed that they have the ability to laugh themselves. They spread wholesome joy and laughter.

Laughing for them, is not merely laughing at others. You won't hear them telling jokes about another 'community' with intentions of ridicule, and, in the process create laughter.

Laughing to the winners does not lie in the misfortunes of others although their own misfortunes are worth telling for a laugh. When there is so much fun in life itself, why make jokes at the expense of others?

You too will laugh with them. It is fun to have them around.

Winners, being individuals who are in touch with reality, accept life. They are people whom you enjoy meeting. They are people you enjoy sharing your life with, and in the process, laugh with.

How would you rate yourself on this count?

My Score	0	1	2	3	4	5

CARAT COUNT NO. 10

Serenity in Accepting Reality

"Not as tall as the current popular film star, but myself." That is the total acceptance of self without any complaints.

A genuine individual shall always consider such prefixes as "If only I was..." a waste of creative energy. What is the use of repeating statements like, "If only my parents were richer," "If only I could be a businessman," "If only I had more educational qualifications," "If only I had a better car," and so many other 'if onlys' that cannot make any changes in the hard realities of life?

They neither know, nor speak about generation gaps. Is it not true that generation gaps have always existed throughout history and shall continue to remain so? Is it really a new, modern phenomenon? Each generation shall think and act differently. And, that is very natural too. So what is this gap that many people seem to make a big scene about? A gap is something that exists within you. And, you are the one who must do something definite to bridge it.

Do any of these people consider practical solutions? Or, are they all so happy blaming someone else for their own inability to understand the current reality, to accept it and act in tune with it?

Winners neither know, nor speak, about generation gaps.

Winning parents do not have much problem with their children. They have developed healthy relationships with their children. And the children too have an excellent rapport with them. All because they have accepted each other.

Winning teachers do not have much problems with their students. Students too find it a joy to attend their classes. They have both developed the rapport to understand each other. There is joy in that togetherness that was initiated and established by the responsible ones, the teachers.

The winning team of a husband and wife do not think of divorce. They have no need for it. They are happily married, because they have accepted each other. They know that such an acceptance of the spouse for what he or she really is, is the first step towards building a healthy, fulfilling marital relationship. Because acceptance comes to them naturally, they cultivate a healthy relationship.

All the tears that may flow from you are not going to create an iota of change in the reality. Winners have no time to complain about what they are not and what they do not possess. No hiding behind artificial facades, no apologising for what they genuinely are, no short-circuiting and in the process, getting charred with guilt.

Winners accept the natural world and enjoy serene living in that world, for what it is worth.

My Score	0	1	2	3	4	5

CARAT COUNT NO. 11

Understand People Naturally
What appears unfathomable, and utterly complex to so many, is simple common sense to the winner.

Take the case of certain successful salespersons. Where others make tremendous efforts to make a sale, and fail, these people do it easily and joyfully. And, the buyer is only too happy that he has bought from them. And, in the process, the salesman also creates lifelong friendship, if he is genuine. Everyone is eager to know, "How did you do that?"

Where one parent tried all the tricks in the book with the kid, and failed, another parent succeeded so joyfully. How?

Have you heard the old adage, "You can lead a thousand horses to water, but you cannot make one of them drink?" But *it is* possible to make those horses drink. First of all, you have to make them thirsty. Then, the horses shall drink on their own. This requires an understanding of horses.

Insight is what is needed; insights gained into the mind and motivations of others through experiences. *"Experience to me is the greatest teacher. I can trust my experience."* That is the philosophy of such successful persons.

Understanding others comes from understanding the self. Not merely through acquiring a Master's degree in psychology.

Truly successful persons count experience in terms of what they learn from life and not merely in terms of the number of years they are alive. *Young in years, but old in wisdom;* they learn while they live.

Are you always aware of what is happening within you in various situations of life? Do you observe your life very closely? Do you watch those inner reactions with the attitude of a witness? If you do, you will know what is happening in others too. Because you know that those things that happen to others do take place within you too. You are aware. This truly is the process of becoming a master of psychology. Not merely through devouring thick textbooks and through certification by others. But, through observing life very closely and understanding people naturally.

Human problems to such winners, even those which immobilise so many others, shall be minor annoyances. They will say of people who pose problems, "Oh! It is only natural they behave that way." And, then, they shall get on with finding the solutions.

Do you understand and accept yourself and others too? Do you make spontaneous efforts to understand people? Are you busy living and winning?

My Score	0	1	2	3	4	5

CARAT COUNT NO. 12

Freedom from Useless Fights

Useless fights. That is what we see all around us.

The couple next door is still at it. It is an everyday affair. Why? I have no clue. I have a feeling that they too have no idea whatsoever.

Everywhere we see these useless fights. Between siblings, between couples, between parents, between employer and employees, between social units, between religious factions, between states, between nations, and I suppose, between gods too.

What is happening in some of the Middle Eastern countries? Conflicts and friction have been going on for years. Some say that the battle is on principles. What principles and whose principles? Is there no better practical way to make those essential fights more meaningful, productive and beneficial?

If fighting will bring progress that is worthwhile, useful and productive, it is definitely necessary to fight fiercely and win in the end. But those definitions of fighting which lead people to think of annihilating the enemy, is a primitive one. By such approaches, nobody really wins; nobody ever won. Both the parties were busy destroying each other. Is that the real definition of winning?

Certainly, winners *have to be* fighters too. They have to engage themselves in a fight that shall not be based on ego gratification or with the intention to destroy others. That is not our definition of winning.

Since you and I, as winners, are not seeking approval, we cannot afford to be busy trying to change the society to suit our own needs. Are we here to force advice on others and to alter their behaviour to suit our own convenience?

A *winner* shall not engage himself or herself in useless fights. Why choose to waste your skill and energy on causes which do not amount to anything worthwhile in reality?

Society's problems do not trouble winners. You'll hear them say, "Oh! That's not my problem. It is his own. Let him do the worrying. Why should I worry for him? When he himself doesn't realise that he has a problem, and, when he is not really keen to solve it, how can I help him?" They will also add, "If he wants my help, and if he asks for it, I shall certainly help him to the best of my capacity."

That's it. "I am not out to engage myself in useless fights. As it is, I am busy solving my own problems."

You must know when to fight and when to lie low. You certainly cannot afford to engage yourself in useless fights.

My Score	0	1	2	3	4	5

CARAT COUNT NO. 13

Freedom from Sickness Syndrome
Think of the time when someone becomes sick and is admitted to a hospital. The convention is that visitors have to come in a

stream, one after another. And, each one will talk more about sickness. That means more sickly people. In the process, the patient himself becomes sicker.

Then there are others. When they are in normal health, nobody gives them a second look. But when they are sick, there are more people around, giving that attention which was needed by them before. Thus, the individual concludes, "It pays to remain sick."

And, very often sickness is a wonderful excuse for not doing the work that I am responsible for. On so many occasions, the student had to make his parents sick so that he was excused from completing his homework. Sickness, thus, pays in many ways.

The result is the *sickness syndrome.*

Winners are not sickly people. They do not let sicknesses such as colds, flu or headaches knock them out. The body, they realise, is a complex mechanism and needs maintenance, preventive or otherwise. But, life and work must go on.

Sickness to a winner is not an excuse for self-pity or to gain sympathy from others. Sickness only means that the body needs maintenance.

Sympathy is negative. It is to be shunned. "My body is sick. I am not." To these people, a healthy body is a responsibility. They know how their bodies respond. They plan to do all that is necessary to keep it in a good working condition.

By choosing to talk about their illnesses, you don't reach far with them. Winners shall not do it to others, or to themselves.

All of us do need love. And, we are dependent on others for that love. But love can never be made out as an excuse to spread sickness. Thus, you and I cannot afford to become a prey to this sickness syndrome.

Winners like to live well and they do.

My Score	0	1	2	3	4	5

CARAT COUNT NO. 14

Free from the Convention Rut
When I was to receive that certificate making me a graduate, I had to wear a weird black gown and an outmoded version of a hat. Why? Conventions say that it has to be done that way. But such clothes are not even seen around today. They are just not

available, but because it is a convention that has been followed for hundreds of years, and if I have to collect the degree from the Chief Guest, then I have to find a black gown. Otherwise, it shall be sent to me by post.

Yet, fashion is a megabuck business today. Millions are being spent on designing and promoting the sale of even underwear. Imagine what would happen if the university prescribes that all graduates must wear that style of undergarment that their great-grandparents wore, otherwise, the degree shall not be granted to them!

You shall find much of these anachronisms everywhere around you. I agree that there are many wonderful things that we can learn from the past. Certainly we must preserve them and benefit from them. I must, most certainly, benefit from the experiences gained by others. But there are some conventions within which we should not get caught up.

Do I have to start and run a business exactly in the same way that my grandfather did? Or, am I supposed to bring about qualitative changes to suit the current needs of the society?

How about dealing with children?

Winners care little for textbook rules. They do not worship conventions. They are rational about conditioning, organisations and systems imposed upon them.

"A system is made by man to win. If it helps you to win, use it. If it does not, make changes and create new approaches. Winning authentically is all that matters." This is the approach of a winner.

All of us have to become 'doers'. We have to be pragmatic. We have to be action-oriented. Not just followers of rules and conventions. We have to learn and benefit from the wisdom of others. We cannot remain blind followers of conventions. Let no one try to bind you with rigid formulae. They shall not be allowed to succeed. Because, you want to win in the end.

Winners are functional and pragmatic. Not dogmatic. To them, nothing succeeds like success. They rely on their experiences. They are flexible enough to adjust and find new systems and approaches. When we shall become free from the *Convention Rut* we will not be required to look at things only in a particular way. We will not have to remain busy consulting manuals and asking expert opinions all the time. We shall begin to apply our imagination in more varied ways and shall achieve creativity of the highest order.

| My Score | 0 | 1 | 2 | 3 | 4 | 5 |

CARAT COUNT NO. 15

Fired by Enthusiasm

We have often been fascinated watching these dynamos at work. They seem to possess all the energy, all the time for the many activities they are engaged in. They are busy rushing, planning, directing, chasing, pushing, getting things done, and, yet have sufficient energy to play tennis, attend parties, read books, write articles, tell stories to their children and attend to a hundred other things. They have located a master switch to high, personal energy level.

The word *enthusiasm* comes from the Greek root *enthousiasmos* which means 'a god-inspired zeal'—*en* means 'in' and *theos* means 'a god'. Thus, it means being highly inspired, of intense interest, of passionate zeal.

Winners are enthusiastic, and being so, their energy levels remain high. Healthy people, they are stirred by an intense fervour towards fulfilment. Because of this, every component of their body responds to the need to aspire to greater heights.

The master switch is always on. The energy flows like the perennial waterfall which never dries up. They do not become bored or tired. They will refuse to engage in a conversation about their tiredness or sickness. They are not Superman either. They have so many worthwhile goals to pursue; they are busy feeling, thinking and doing, engaged in the present moment activity. Out of this zeal, they receive a boundless supply of power to live life fully.

Boredom is not in the lives of winners because they clearly know the way to dispatch their energy into productive paths, where most others are directing them into pathways that are useless, unproductive and worthless.

They drink from the fountain of youth. They have all the energy. They are busy living, busy working and busy winning. They don't get old, tired, haggard, exhausted or bedridden. They depart when the call comes. To die is human. We all do.

But while winners live, they tap the powerhouse that was quietly functioning at the highest levels of efficiency. When they die, they too shall be buried unlike most others, who were *dead at 30, but buried at 70.*

My Score	0	1	2	3	4	5

CARAT COUNT NO. 16

Continuous Curiosity and Discovery

Winners are like children. The fascination the world holds for them, the wonder and curiosity are still present in them. Creative responses, liveliness and growth are their constant companions. They have a spontaneous curiosity towards everything they touch or come in contact with during working hours.

They realise the value of discovery. In their daily explorations, they stumble repeatedly upon new relationships among seemingly unrelated things. And once they have seen these, they never seem to tire of reviewing them too.

Winners are not afraid to ask a lady of the house how she keeps her floor so clean and tidy. Or asking a shopkeeper how he remembers the personal preferences of so many individual customers. Or to question a beggar how it feels to be seeking alms all day long. Or to enquire from a worker why the nut should turned clockwise and the wheel anti-clockwise.

They react spontaneously and with avid interest to impressions, with a rapt sense of wonder, attention to minute details and sheer poetic intensity of living. They possess the divine discontent.

They are happy individuals. Very much so. But, they don't accept things merely on face value.

They are unhappy with the way things are because they are keen to improve the quality of their own lives as well as that of others.

They are curious, aggressively so. They are learning, continuously and meaningfully so. They are challenging, menacingly so. They are busy seeking the truth, excited about discovering more and never believing that they themselves are finished products. They are busy in the pursuit of excellence.

If they are near a cook, they want to learn more about cooking. They learn from children, from parents, from the street showmen, from their spouses too. They want to know more about biscuit-making, metal-printing, gas-welding or running the Municipal Administration. They have never learned enough.

They won't teach you, although they might choose to share with you. They are teachers of that variety who believe in learning themselves, becoming self-sufficient in their knowing, and then helping others wherever possible.

To winners, every person, every object, every event represents an opportunity to learn more and become happy in the process. And they are dynamic in their pursuit of learning.

Every day to a winner, is an exciting, enriching and enlightening learning experience.

My Score	0	1	2	3	4	5

CARAT COUNT NO. 17

Unafraid to Fail

An American professor who was on a lecture tour in India, was speaking about the popularity of various training seminars in the USA. It is often beyond the comprehension of most Indians that thousands or millions of people can spend such large amounts of money and time, and participate in them. Aren't most of these seminars selling the same wines in different bottles?

The professor had an interesting reply to offer. "Maybe. Maybe not. But the way to really know is only through first-hand experience." And then he added, "Americans, in general, are not afraid to make mistakes. You may say they have lots of money to throw about. That's not true. No one, leave alone the Americans has any money to throw about. Whenever anything new is offered, they are generally not scared to test it out. Even if it was a waste of money, they would like to know it to be true from personal knowledge."

Nothing is learned without attempting, without sticking the neck out. And to fail is not a crime. It is a part of the learning experience.

Winners are not afraid to fail.

When someone else says, "You have failed," it does not mean a thing to a winner. That is another person's opinion. "I have not failed nor won just because someone else says so. I win only when I accept so. I fail too, only when I consider so. Only I know what will bring about a win. I have set my own goals. I know what is useful, worthwhile and productive. I pursue my goals. How can others judge me?"

"I also know," they will continue in the same tone, "that obstacles and setbacks are part of the winning process. If someone else says that I have failed, it doesn't mean that I have failed. If others think that I have failed, that is their problem. Not mine."

Failures, too, are an essential part of growing up. Winners are not upset by temporary setbacks. They are not afraid to take those essential chances.

My Score	0	1	2	3	4	5

CARAT COUNT NO. 18

Free from Defensiveness
We have to understand the utter futility of defending ourselves in front of those who are determined not to listen. " We know very well that you are a crook. Prove to us that you are not." Could you ever prove anything to such people? What could possibly be the gains from such a defensive pursuit?

"Difficult to practise," you may say. "How can anyone remain silent when his prestige is being challenged?"

"But when they deliberately turn a deaf ear, what can you do? What shall you gain by defending yourself?"

Socrates, the great master, was being tried by the same sort of people. It was immaterial whether he defended himself or not, for they had come prepared to convict him, to make him drink the hemlock.

What is the use of talking to a judge who has already signed his judgment awarding the sentence of punishment?

What benefit can the young man hope to gain by arguing his case to the Personnel Manager who has already issued the appointment order for the only vacant post to someone else?

When someone taunts you saying, 'You have an inferiority complex,' what is the use arguing with him that it is not so?

Here is an extract from an exclusive interview with Shri Satya Sai Baba published in *The Free Press Journal*, Bombay dated May 20, 1979:

Question: There had been from time to time, criticism about you in a section of the press. Some people have also challenged you. Yet, you have refrained from giving any reply of any kind. Any comment?

Sri Satya Sai Baba: I have remained silent because I have not felt the need for any reply. My conscience is clear and I know fully well that they—the critics—are accusing me of things which I know very well, are totally untrue. Why should I bother about such statements? It is like being told I am bald. Then, why should I counter a statement which, I know, is false?

Secondly, when I see my own Self in the whole of the universe around me, to take note of criticism and enter into argument would be to descend to the place of duality.

Here is the bold truth. Winners have realised it. Mark it, remember it and learn to handle it. There are always many people who would love to see you slip, see you suffer misfortune, see you get into real light spots, see you lose money or miss out on promotions.

They feel happy telling you, 'I told you so,' or 'He got what he deserved,' or 'He always thought too highly about himself. Now look at him.' Yes! There are people, and there are many of them, who take a wicked, wicked delight in seeing a person being CRUCIFIED.

What is the use of a defensive posture in front of them?

When someone goes on complaining about you intermittently, and you do not offer any replies, the hearers are going to ask: "Why does he not choose to defend himself? Maybe the accusation itself is false."

Learning how to handle belittlers, critics and related classes of petty people come naturally to winners. They know there is no need to defend themselves or their actions.

My Score	0	1	2	3	4	5

CARAT COUNT NO. 19

Freedom from Boundary Bondage

There are so many boundaries that are created by the human race behind by which they isolate themselves. These boundaries become fetters that prevent people from reaching out into the human world. These tend to condition people to develop a narrow-minded outlook. And this results in quarrels, selfishness, insensitivity towards others and all the wars.

Winners are not limited people. They do not identify merely with their own family, their language, their neighbourhood, their community, their village, their state, their country or their nation. An unemployed Punjabi is no better or worse than an unemployed Maharashtrian. A starving Vietnamese is no different from a poverty-stricken Sudanese. Nor, for that matter, an African, an American, a Chinese or a Sri Lankan.

They do not practise parochialism in the guise of patriotism. Winners are ready to help others, irrespective of their background.

If a person is hurt in an accident, they do not choose to verify his language or caste before giving a little help. Winners understand that in truth there is only one language, the language that binds the human race as one.

Winners do not feel any special joy to see that an enemy is harmed or killed. There are no enemies. There are only people. Some of them behave in ways that are different from those of the winner. That doesn't make them enemies. Those divisions which are drawn by some men to keep others out are not for winners to observe. They just do not accept those traditional boundaries which cause people to label others as rebels, traitors, non-religious, undesirables, untouchables, blacks, browns or whites. They, like gold, are univalent as well as trivalent.

Food to them is food, be it South Indian, Mughlai, Continental or Chinese. They love and relish all kinds of foods. They have a special liking for certain items of food of course, as it is only human to have preferences. But that is no reason for a winner to be addicted to one and dismiss all others as undesirable.

If they go to a distant country and have to make do with foods other than their favourite ones, they are not going to starve. Nor are they going to continually disapprove.

If they see social customs which are different from their own, they do not go all out to disapprove. It is only natural that different people behave in different ways.

Not contained within boundaries, winners thrive everywhere, with everything and with everyone.

They soar high and are free.

My Score	0	1	2	3	4	5

CARAT COUNT NO. 20

Clear Priority of Values

In a complex, technological, modern era, we see many members of society who do not practise what they preach. High-sounding declarations on moral values, dedication to duty, adherence to principles, non-acceptance of gifts, not coveting others' properties and other such pronouncements are being spoken about from high pedestals. In actual practice, to these same people, cleanliness is throwing dirt out of the windows. To them, corrupt people are only those other than themselves. And, snatching away the properties of others is their path to making more money.

We see leaders encouraging austerity through public speeches, and yet spending millions on vulgar displays before the public, during private celebrations.

The one who always preaches about honesty, we have observed, is often the one who needs to be paid under the table if our legitimate work has to get going. As far as I am concerned, the basic question here is, *How can I accept an additional payment from someone else for performing my legitimate duties, for which I am already paid by my employer?*

What people often practise is in direct contrast to what they preach.

Winners clearly know the priority of their values. They know their limitations, and what they are engaged in.

If they enjoy getting up late in the mornings, they know they are doing it with self-approval. No amount of your sermons on 'Purposeful Living' is going to make even an iota of change in their priorities. If they feel the need to change priorities, they certainly can and will do it. But when they do, it will not be merely because someone else has been telling them to do so.

If you tell them, 'You must not allow your children to watch movies. They are bad for their growth,' they will agree with you and insist that *YOU* must continue to behave in the way you preach.

Personally, I have been watching movies right from my childhood, and, I still do. I don't think they have spoiled me or my parents. Maybe I was fortunate that my parents had instilled much better values within me before I was exposed to movies. Today, I pick up only those values that have a meaning and purpose to my growth as a human being. All others are rejected outright.

You need to be clear about what you are doing, so that you can continue to act in ways that you choose. And, when needed, you should also be willing to alter your choices deliberately.

Being observant, winners become aware of realities. They see no conflicts. They do not feel the need to change their own basic nature.

As for the society, the right thing is what the society is practising and not what it is merely preaching.

There are *Individual Values* and *Social Values*. We cannot afford to have any confusion on this account. When dealing with the society, we have to learn to arrive at *Workable Compromises*, become pragmatic, practical, and powerful individuals.

To be a winner, we shall define a *Value* as something that is freely chosen from alternatives and is acted upon, and that which we can celebrate as being part of our creative integration during our development as a person. We shall choose our values deliberately, arrange their priorities and shall continue to act upon them. (More about this later.)

We have to become experts in our Resource Management and Time Management. We have so many things to do. As such, we shall arrange our work according to our priorities and shall remain busy doing those tasks or activities that are high in a list of priorities.

When we feel the need for a bit of diversion, we may even choose to engage ourselves in harmless gossip. But unlike many others, the difference shall lie in the fact that we shall not make gossiping a full-time activity.

Winners have no conflict watching the society at work nor living within it. When you too shall choose to be a winner, you too shall know your *Values* as well your *Priorities* clearly.

My Score	0	1	2	3	4	5

CARAT COUNT NO. 21

Brutally Honest

The meaning of honesty is *not* clearly understood by most people.

Let us take an example.

I was visiting an old man in the intensive care unit of a hospital. He had been struck by a heart attack a few days ago. As he was speaking to me, he inquired about his home, asking "How is my family?", "How is my son?"

I was in a dilemma as his son had been involved in a motorcycle accident two days ago and was laid up in another hospital with multiple fractures. Now, you tell me, what I should have told the old man?

If honesty only means to speak the truth as it is, it will only create more problems and complications.

Before I answer the question, let us try to arrive at the meaning of this word. If you are willing to reflect, you too will understand and practise *honesty* as a quality which is *just, candid, truthful, chaste, free-from-fraud, fair* and *honourable*. Thus, honesty should also be related to purpose.

What should my purpose have been while answering this sick, old man about his son? You may decide on the answer that you may give. But, for me, the answer shall be, "Fine. Now you take care, and get well soon." Check this answer against the definition of honesty.

Now, honesty is not merely stating a fact as it is without any consideration of the effect it may have on others. If you check my answer, you will see that it relates to every component of the definition of the word.

Thus, another hallmark of these fully functioning individuals, is their honesty. They have no pretensions, no evasive responses, and no lies to propagate. They see uttering a lie as self-deception and distortion of their own reality.

They know that they are in charge of themselves. They realise that they can behave only in the way they naturally are. To others, winners might sometimes appear cruel because of the ruthless way they take charge of themselves, and accept responsibility for their own actions.

How would you rate yourself about your understanding and practice of honesty?

My Score	0	1	2	3	4	5

CARAT COUNT NO. 22

Clarity on Long-Range Goals

A goal or an objective is a well-defined end result. To have a goal means to be able to see the end product clearly. Every end product is made up of so many separate actions, often appearing unconnected, but always made in the *Here and Now*.

Take the case of students. Generally, they enjoy doing many other things, rather than sitting down and studying. Studying is very boring for most of them. But what about that student who has regular, well laid out schedules for studying, and who adheres to them too? While there are so many other fascinating distractions around him, how does he manage to complete his studies too? The answer has to be found in his long-range goals. These inspire him to carry on.

Take the businessman who is putting up an industry. Take the accountant who has to draw up a balance sheet. Take that physician who has to keep on listening to the same complaints all over again from his sick patients. Take the film director who has to complete making the film and release it on the due date. In all these cases, to be successful it is essential to have a clarity of long-range goals.

Winning (like film-making) can be very boring, if viewed only as a general activity. Most of us who went to watch our favourite film stars perform in front of the camera, came back disappointed. The pace was very slow and almost nothing was happening. But to the director who was involved and could visualise the finished product, a film is made up of so many single shots, while every frame has to fit properly within the overall long-range goal. As the director knows this, the work itself becomes an exciting proposition to him.

Winners shall have their goals properly defined, and set. They shall also have checked that their goals are practical, attainable, worthwhile, clearly stated, compatible and measurable.

When the winner shall say, *"Rome was not built in a day,"* they shall not be merely repeating an old proverb. They are reflecting on their commitment towards goals which are to be realised in the future, but shall be made up of the actions performed in the *here and now* moments.

Equipped with a navigation chart and a rudder to steer with, winners shall be intensely aware that their destination is far, and sailing continuously has to be accepted before the goal is reached. They shall have a *vision* that is clearly focussed.

My Score	0	1	2	3	4	5

CARAT COUNT NO. 23

Freedom from Envy

Winners are free from envy and heart-burning at the achievements of others.

Envy has an almost opposite effect to that of having goals.

Goals inspire people towards achievements.

Envy leads people to think of ways to prevent others from achieving their goals.

Goals direct the physical energy into constructive directions.

Envy shall direct those in destructive ways.

Goals lead to progressive attainments.

Envy does not have any basis for attainments. Its only concern is about preventing others from attainments.

Goals generate positive approaches.

Envy generates negative approaches.

A person with goals shall be inspired towards accomplishing something worthwhile, productive and useful.

Envy shall only provoke the person to think of unworthy, unproductive and useless pursuits.

A person with goals shall be serene and joyful.

Those with envy shall be agitated and unhappy.

Winners do not waste their creative energy demanding justice from the society. When someone else enjoys more privileges, it is not a reason for them to become unhappy. They do not want an opponent to underplay his part so that the winner can get to feel that he is winning.

Winners choose to win through their own efforts, rather than gaining advantages through the shortcomings of others.

They do not demand equality for all. Equality to them is a myth. Happiness can be achieved only by locating it within. They are no critics, they are no grumblers, nor are they *keepers-up-with-the Joneses*. They are busy living. They have no time or inclination to get burned thinking about what others *are* or what others *are doing*.

Having succeeded in preventing jealousy from finding a place within, winners are constantly seeking fulfilment as they aim towards goals that are positive and creative.

My Score	0	1	2	3	4	5

CARAT COUNT NO. 24

Love and Respect for Self

Most significantly, a winner is an individual who loves himself. A winner does not see any reasons at all for *self-hate, self-pity, self-contempt, or self-rejection.*

Motivated by a desire to grow, they treat themselves with respect and love. When you ask them "How do you do?" they will tell you, "Great! Wonderful! Nothing could be better." They are essentially speaking about themselves and about what is happening within them.

"If I do not respect myself, how can others do it?" And they are right. "Before I can expect others to love and respect me, I must do so myself." That's their philosophy. Not out of conceit, but of the recognition that every individual is made in the image of the divine.

They are not problem-free. They too have their share of troubles and worries. Only the dead do not have problems.

They are happy because they can accept themselves.
They have accepted themselves and are happy.

They are the Winners.

My Score	0	1	2	3	4	5

Success and Personal Development

Those who cannot project their personality acceptably, do not think or reflect in private. That is the problem.

The word is a disorderly place, and it has always been so. The person who wants to make the best of his or her life, must learn to live in it comfortably.

It is one thing to have some sense of order within. But it is quite another to bring about the order through conscious, positive efforts.

When more and more people shall realise this truth, and shall continue to strive towards excellence, the world too would have become a happier place to live in.

To that day, *Cheers!*

Now, enter your score as on today in the next page, and, add up your score. Do this exercise all over again carefully, after 6 months. You could be pleasantly surprised.

24 Carats of Winning Personality—Where do I stand today?

Carat No.	Description	My Score Today	After 6 Months (mention dates)
1	Uniqueness		
2	Capacity to Enjoy, to Laugh		
3	Freedom from Excuses and Guilt		
4	Freedom from Anxiety, Tension, Worry		
5	Living in the Present, Here and Now		
6	Self-reliant, Self-dependent		
7	Freedom from Approval Seeking		
8	Clarity on Social Values		
9	Laughing and Spreading Joy		
10	Serenity to Accept Reality		
11	Understands People Naturally		
12	Freedom from Useless Fights		
13	Freedom from 'Sickness Syndrome'		
14	Freedom from Conventions Rut		
15	Fired by Enthusiasm		
16	Continuous Curiosity and Discovery		
17	Unafraid to Fail		
18	Free from Defensiveness		
19	Free from Boundary Bondage		
20	Clear Priority of Values		
21	Brutally Honest		
22	Clarity on Long-Range Goals		
23	Freedom from Envy		
24	Love and Respect for Self		

8

Others Only Echo What We Whisper to Them in Silence

> *"A calf can find its mother cow*
>   *Among a thousand kine:*
> *So is the Good or the Evil done, returns*
>   *And whispers: 'I am thine.'*
> —PANCHATANTRA

In the island of Cyprus, in Amathus, there lived a sculptor named Pygmalion. Passionately devoted to his art, Pygmalion was only happy in the silent world of statues which his chisel had created. Those were the days when the girls of Amathus had rashly denied the divinity of Aphrodite, the Greek goddess of love.

To punish those girls, Aphrodite instilled such immodesty in them that, losing all sense of shame, they prostituted themselves to all comers. In the end, they were turned into rocks.

Pygmalion, being an admirer of Aphrodite, thus shunned any association with women. But, he fervently venerated Aphrodite. Now, it came about that he made an ivory statue of a woman and named it Galatea. That statue was of such extraordinary beauty that he fell in love with it. He began to wish, "If only it was alive." Alas! The cold image did not respond to his transports of love.

Aphrodite took pity on this singular lover. One day, while he was pressing the inert statue in his arms, Pygmalion felt the ivory suddenly moving and his kisses were returned. The statue became miraculously alive.

From this beautiful Greek tale, George Bernard Shaw created one of the loveliest stories ever told, *Pygmalion*. It was celebrated on the stage and when it was made into a movie, it became an all-time hit by the name of *My Fair Lady*.

There is a valuable lesson we can learn from this beautiful story. To know it better, let us look at the storyline of Shaw's *Pygmalion*.

Professor Higgins, a bachelor, had picked up Eliza Doolittle, a dirty, uncivilised, flower-vendor from the marketplace on a bet with Colonel Pickering. Higgins was determined to turn that ugly little flower girl into a beautiful lady and pass her off as a duchess in the Embassy Ball.

In the course of their long interaction, Higgins, the staunch bachelor, was unknowingly falling in love with Eliza.

After Higgins had won his bet, he and Eliza had one of their quarrels. Eliza left the house, and went to Mrs. Higgins, the mother of our professor, with a complaint: *"You see,"* said the Fair Lady, *"really and truly apart from the things anyone can learn (the dress, the tone, the manner and the etiquette), the difference between a flower girl and a duchess is not how she behaves, but how she is treated by others. I shall always be a flower girl to Higgins because he always treats me as such and always will. But I know I shall be a duchess to Colonel Pickering because he treats me with respect and dignity. He is a gentleman."*

Again, from this charming tale, came the psychological concept of what is popularly known as the 'Pygmalion Effect'. It is also called a 'Self-fulfilling Prophesy'. The expectations we hold about a person's behaviour, often serve as factors for fulfilling those very expectations.

A classic example is that of the 'Pygmalion Effect in a Classroom'. When the new teacher comes to the class with fear and trepidation about facing the students, signals go out from the teacher to the students spurring them to misbehave. When children, on the other hand, are made to feel that they have unusual potential for growth, they in turn gain significantly in their I.Q. too.

Students do not misbehave with all their teachers. Only with some of them. What makes this difference?

What happened to you when in a certain event you expected to succeed, and you did so?

Or in situations where you chose to feel defensive and you were surely pushed with your back to the wall.

What about that time when you wanted something very badly in your life, and you went ahead and did everything in your power to get it, and finally achieved your goal?

When people approach their work thinking negatively, they land up with failure. Such people do not realise that those things which *'we whisper to the silence of others'* shall always be returned to us in full measure. It is of utmost importance for us to choose that correct frame of mind when dealing with problems and difficulties.

SELF-FULFILLING PROPHESIES

Mahesh Desai, an electronics engineer, became the partner of a firm at the death of his father. His senior partner, an elderly gentleman, was a great friend of his father and also a prominent manufacturer of electronic components.

Mahesh *felt* that he was being criticised unjustly and his best jobs were often rejected. He also felt that his partner was being deliberately rude and unfair to him. And this led to Mahesh harbouring a deep resentment within himself about his partner.

Fortunately, before things could go out of hand, he and his partner had an open dialogue which led to creating a better understanding and trust.

During moments of contemplation, Mahesh realised that in his mind, he had always been attributing unfair motives to his partner. Automatically, his partner too was establishing reciprocal negative behaviour patterns towards Mahesh. Luckily, unlike in many other cases, before it was too late, Mahesh realised the role and the significance of the 'Pygmalion Effect'. After a long, frank chat with his senior partner, he was ready to sort out his problems easily.

When Mahesh changed his thoughts about his partner 'Uncle', his job became highly enjoyable. His relationship too became a happier one.

NOT FACTS, BUT IMAGINATION

Many of us do not face others directly. Preconceived ideas are so fixed in our minds, that we lose out much in life unknowingly.

It is not facts but the imagination that creates and shapes our lives. When we understand this properly, our lives too will shape more profitably.

Take P.K. Purohit, for example. Even when we first met him, he was brilliant. You only had to sit with him and slowly tune in. It took a little time, but then you could hear so many brilliant statements from him. He was amazing. He was so clear about what he had to offer.

But when he had to be in the company of unknown people, he was woefully inadequate. You could never see a worse shape of living flesh in abject misery. It took Purohit a few weeks to come to terms with his problems, and all those childhood beliefs and attitudes. He feared that every person was there to grab him and pack him into a briefcase to be whisked away into that land from where children never returned. Probably someone had used a trick to keep him from crying when he was a little toddler.

It took him a few weeks to change. All we had to do was to change his frame of mind.

We made a *Descriptive Statement* and an *Affirmation* for him. We made him read them loud. Each time he did, his mental outlook was being changed from negative to positive. He is brilliant today. The moment you look at him, you will respond to him positively.

Here is the text of the *Affirmation*, in case you would like to know what it is:

I benefit from meeting people and interacting with them. My confidence in myself benefits me greatly, especially in my work.

I see myself interacting pleasantly with people. I am well-informed on topics that I have studied, because I have spent many hours learning about them. As I interact with others, my ideas flow well and I see myself enjoying the experience. Several people offer me congratulations, making me feel important and worthy.

Affirmation: *I AM A CONFIDENT AND SUCCESSFUL PERSON.*

How would I rate myself today on my understanding and practice of *Self-fulfilling Prophesies?*

My Score	0	1	2	3	4	5

9

Art: An Aid in Understanding the World

> "It requires more than a day's devotion to know and to possess the wealth of a day."
> — HENRY DAVID THOREAU
> American poet, naturalist, essayist
>
> "For art comes to you, proposing frankly to give you nothing but the highest quality to your moments as they pass."
> — WALTER PATER
> "The Renaissance"

WHAT IS ART?

Probably no term has been so widely discussed with so unclear a definition.

Until the eighteenth century, it became customary to group certain arts under the heading of the Fine and Beautiful

Arts. Around the same time, the idea came to be accepted that these fine arts are the products of genius whose methods cannot be reduced to any known rules or principles. This idea was developed until art was thought to defy any systematic approach to its creation. And the term began to be used in a sense almost opposite in meaning to the older definition.

As a result, since the beginning of the nineteenth century, art has been spoken of frequently as though it were too lofty and esoteric. That made it difficult to comprehend or to make it amenable to close examination.

First of all, and most broadly, art is an aid in understanding the world. It may be compared to history, philosophy or science, which attempt to formalise or discover, and record patterns in man's experience. Art may deal with the same subject matter as these other approaches. It may even use some of the same methods. For example, history seems to record the facts of man's past. But as it cannot report everything about living from day to day, it tends to select those facts which seem significant and which appear to compose a pattern of cause and effect. Thus, history, like art, *selects, arranges, and gives emphasis to its materials.*

Philosophy seeks to find the truths and principles underlying all beings and relate them to human existence.

A drama or a discourse too may seek to suggest answers to such a quest. Such branches of science as psychology and sociology seek to determine the causes and probabilities of certain kinds of behaviour.

Mostly, when a person interacts with others, especially in these modern times, he is bound to have some of these concerns. Each approach to man's experience attempts to discover and understand the self and the world in which he lives.

There are always significant differences in the methods used by various approaches. History, philosophy and science attempt to set their conclusions down in logical expository prose. A point of view is expressed, and proof is marshalled to support that view and to gain its acceptance.

These methods are directed principally to the intellect.

But the *Personality Development* and the *Personality Projection* that we are discussing, attempts to work through direct involvement of the other person's emotions, imagination and intellect, and by presenting experience directly. For example, when we speak or when we perform a drama, what we say illumines and comments on human experience, and at the same time, appears to create human experience. While speaking, you can narrate events as though they are occurring at that moment before your eyes. We tend to absorb those events as we absorb life itself—through their direct impact on our senses. The art element here strips away all irrelevant details and organises events so that they compose a significant, meaningful pattern.

Another distinguishing characteristic of this art lies in its manipulation of the imagination.

As a salesman, even while speaking about a machine, you tend to make an imaginative recreation of events and performance. The personal actions are defined and dialogues are invented. The other person is made to experience a historical event, even when he realises that what takes place is only a fictional version of the original.

THE APPROACH

Each art form uses a different group of techniques. In the process, they become equipped to deal with a particular aspect of human experience.

Music for example, uses rhythm, melody, and expresses stages of feeling. We value music not so much for what it 'says' as for what it 'does' to us. It may calm or excite. Whenever it engages our attention, we are involved in it and respond to its rhythmic patterns.

The more completely our attention is engaged, the less are we conscious of other factors outside the musical experience. At such times we work or dance without being aware of our efforts. Our energies are released. We gain a sense of freedom, power and inner harmony. It is only after the music is stopped that we become aware of the fatigue and frustration. During the musical experience itself, those states and stages of feelings expressed in terms of time and sound become the centre of our existence.

Art: An Aid in Understanding the World

Music, then, as an art form, makes its appeal through the ear. It organises sound and time into feeling states which relate to our basic patterns of sensation.

Paintings make their appeal through the eyes, formalising man's relationship to space. Line, mass and colour are used to create pleasing compositions. They express both order and harmony of emotions and perceptions. The content may or may not represent real-life objects. Though recognisable subject matter may add another source of pleasure for the viewer, the essential appeal in a painting does not lie in its ability to produce an exact likeness. Rather, it allows man to experience and understand spatial relationships.

Art, then, is one way of *ordering, clarifying* and *understanding experience*. Each art form uses its own special techniques. But each manages to express itself in ways which offer both significance and pleasure at the same time.

Your *Personality* is an art form that is most intimately and closely related to the patterns of life and normal living experiences. It is also an art form that is closest to encompassing all of the other arts.

THE PROBLEM OF VALUE IN ART

Art to many may not appear to be useful. It does not produce (they argue or think) the obvious benefits offered by say, medicine or engineering or business. They are convinced that it does not contribute to the progress of civilisations. To many, when compared to business, it seems impractical. Its purposes, thus, remain vague. It becomes fundamentally unimportant to many. (Are you at this moment wondering why I am writing all this in a book on Personality Development? Are you thinking of skipping over this part and jumping on to the next chapter? Do you see the problem of even speaking about the value of art? Wait. Don't skip this page. You will benefit by reading on.)

The financially successful artist is frequently honoured not because he is a good artist, but because he has become successful in a business sense.

Art is an approach to human experience. And those products which are created from this viewpoint must be dealt with as attempts of art. *Personality interactions* are a part of that human experience.

How would I rate myself today on my understanding and practice of *Art: As an aid to understanding the world?*

My Score	0	1	2	3	4	5

10

Making Sense

> "None lacking shrewdness flatter well;
> None but a lover plays the swell;
> No saints are found in judgment seats,
> No clear, straightforward person cheats."
> —Panchatantra

Whether we know it or not, we are all capable of creating meaningful patterns in life. We may not always be reasonable. But, one of the fundamental elements in our power, is to reason. We have the ability to distinguish truth from error.

Rene Descartes (1596–1650), the great French mathematician and philosopher, received the best education his time could offer. Yet, he was disgusted with the results. Therefore, he broke off from the Scholastic Traditions and set out to build himself on a foundation of his own; a foundation which was the beginning of modern philosophy. He tells us: *"It has been my singular good fortune to have, very early in my life, found a methodical way of life."*

His method, quoted from 'Discourse on Method', involves four simple percepts:

1. Never to accept anything as true which you do not clearly know to be such. *Avoid hasty judgements and prejudices.*
2. Divide each difficulty under examination into as many parts as possible, or, into as many as necessary for the solution of the problem.
3. Begin with things that are simplest and easiest to understand. Then ascend to the knowledge of the more complex ones.
4. Make your enumerations so complete, and reviews so comprehensive, that you may be assured that nothing is omitted.

Conclusions arrived by Rene Descartes point to an encouraging thesis:

We are all capable of understanding by using the right approach to thinking.

Yet, it is unfortunately true that we often believe in what we *want to* believe, regardless of reality, or some unconscious interests such as pride or vanity.

It is impossible to convince a person when he has *prejudices* so deeply rooted that he is beyond the reach of rational analysis.

Although all of us are capable of being logical, we often develop bad habits of thinking in certain ways which cloud our judgement. Is it not difficult to think logically in those fields which involve our *emotions* and *self-interest*?

We often forget that we ought to exercise our critical powers. We become dogmatic. We do make definite and arrogant assertions without proof.

People do become blind fanatics, and stop thinking altogether. They become blind followers of authorities. They even stop inquiring whether the pronouncements that are being made can be justified by clear proof. (Let us respect the experts. But, let us not follow them blindly.)

And above all, provincialism or narrow-mindedness make us to regard any ideas other than our own as *outlandish*, or *perverse*, or *dangerous*, or *subversive*.

Nothing is more dangerous than a wholesome scepticism. Life, to most of us, become intolerable without a positive belief in something. And, those persons without any positive beliefs, usually lend themselves as easy preys to the first dogmatist who comes along.

Instead of doubting everything, we could believe those that are backed by sufficient evidence. We could suspend judgments when evidence is lacking. In other words, we could be *Critical-minded* rather than being *Negative-minded*.

SEMANTICS

Semantics is a new word, particularly to most of us in India. It is a study of words (and symbols generally) in relation to their meanings. Words are signs or symbols that usually stand for something other than themselves.

The subject itself is not new. But it was only in the last seventy years or so that *semantics* has emerged as a full-fledged discipline.

Semantics is concerned with language to the extent language is relevant to problems of thinking, understanding and communicating. Words are mysterious things. They are events in space and time. They are physical things.

When we say words have meanings, we say that human beings agree that a certain word, like 'bread' for example, shall refer to a certain physical object. This object could have been called by other names too, as it happens in other languages. But, people generally tend to think that a word is necessarily connected with a certain thing and even find it difficult to refer to it by any other name.

Words can have as many meanings as people give them. A 'spring' may be a season, a source of water or a metal coil.

Knowing about semantics will help us to think more clearly within the self, between man and man, and facilitate better understanding.

CONCLUSION

Even the best methods demand involvement and testing them in experience.

Many years ago, Socrates taught his disciples: "A life not worth examining, is not worth living." Stated more positively, it will read, *A life worth examining, is worth living*. An examined path leads to your enlightenment and brings illumination in the place of darkness.

A *winner* is a human being who is committed to shed light in people's lives, *his own* as well as that of *others*.

How would I rate myself today on my understanding and practice of *Making Sense*?

My score	0	1	2	3	4	5

11

Conviction Commands Commitment

> "For verily I say unto you, that whosoever shall say unto this mountain, be thou removed, and be thou cast into the sea; and shall not doubt in his heart, but shall believe that those things which he sayeth shall come to pass, he shall have whatsoever he sayeth."
>
> —Jesus Christ

Many of us have this problem of CONVICTION. If you want your life to be successful and happy, you have to carry conviction within you.

If we want to get commitment from others, we must carry conviction in our dealings with them.

We have to often fight, if we have to win. Yes! We have to fight with the belief that we shall win.

One of the most inspiring victories in World War II was that of the sinking of the German Battleship Bismarck. The giant

German vessel had become the biggest threat to the Allied naval forces. British intelligence learned that the Bismarck was leaving the North Sea area and was headed for the open sea. It was almost certain that the ship would have many field days sinking British and American ships.

When Winston Churchill learned of this, he made a decision: The Bismarck had to be sunk. His staff officers advised him that this could not be done. The logic of the moment showed that the British obviously lacked ships, aircraft, and the ammunition to do the job.

But all the negative talk did not discourage Churchill. He was determined to win.

Listen to this authentic account of Winston Churchill's conversation with the Fleet Flag Office. This was reported in *Saturday Evening Post*, under the title, "The Last Nine Days of the Bismarck", by C.S. Forester on November 15, 22 and 29, 1958:

From out of the box came the unmistakable tones of the Prime Minister's voice. "Your job is to sink the Bismarck. That is your overriding duty. No other considerations are to have any weight whatever."

"Yes, Mr. Prime Minister."

"What about Ramillies? What about Rodney?"

"Orders are being issued at this moment, Mr. Prime Minister."

"Revenge Force?"

"They have their orders."

"You are taking every possible step to see that the Bismarck is going to be sunk?"

"Yes, Mr. Prime Minister."

"Not only the possible steps, not only the easy steps, and the obvious steps, but the difficult steps and the almost impossible steps, and all the quite impossible steps you can manage as well. The eyes of the whole world are upon us."

"You don't have to remind us about that, Mr. Prime Minister."

"Well, remember. Sink the Bismarck. Goodbye."

History records that Bismarck was sunk. It was quite a battle. But the Bismarck was sunk.

That is an excellent example of conviction in action for us.

Conviction comes from two Latin words; Con means within and Vincere means to conquer. To conquer within. To arrive at a point where there are no doubts within. To ensure that there are no chances whatsoever that a doubt can lodge itself within the mind of the person and remain to stay on there.

In the example cited above, Winston Churchill never gave any chance whatsoever to the listener to express any doubts. Churchill himself did not allow any doubts within himself. He had conquered himself before he gave his specific orders.

Look at the way a successful Sales Manager speaks to his sales team:

"Good morning to you, gentlemen. I am happy to meet all of you this morning. I called you here to remind you about your responsibility to get the CFI order the day after tomorrow. It is a must."

"Someone may influence you by saying that the B S company is doing all sorts of things to get this deal in their favour. But you have only one responsibility tomorrow. Get that order.

"Are your presentation charts ready?" (Yes.) "What about the cost projections?" (All ready, sir.) "Have you got the blueprints for conveyor modifications?" (Yes. They are ready.) "Now remember, Banerjee, Dhawan and Mohan. This is a very important order. It is going to bring a lot of credit to our branch. It is critically important.

"You are in the field. You know what is to be done. You have full freedom to do whatever you consider right. You are to get this contract. Everything is in our favour. I know you can do it." (We are ready, sir.) "Now listen carefully. We have got all the advantages in our favour. So get the order." (Very good, sir. We'll get it.) "That's the spirit. Goodbye, gentlemen."

CONVICTION AND MOTIVATION

From doubts, uncertainty, excuses and willingness to accept failure, the team was taught to be sure, certain and committed. In fact, in both these examples, the full meaning of conviction was made perfectly clear to others.

A winner shall always think and speak with conviction. It is necessary to arrive at a point where all doubts within have been eliminated.

Here it is, step-by-step, a sure way to get an affirmative response and desired results. Apply this conviction to your work, in your conversations, in your day-to-day interactions. See how it promotes commitment, builds morale and gets positive results.

1. *Define precisely the key result area.*
    "Your job is to sink the Bismarck."
    "You have one responsibility tomorrow. Get that order."
    "Reduce the cost by 7 per cent."

"Get that report by 3 p.m."

2. *Speak and act your part with conviction."*

"No other considerations are to have any weight whatsoever."

"This business is absolutely vital for us."

"You will reach the site by 8.30 a.m."

"I shall be waiting for your call at 4.00 p.m."

3. *Ensure that necessary steps have been taken.*

"You're taking every possible step to see that the Bismarck is sunk?"

"Are your presentation charts ready? What about cost projections?"

"Have you personally checked that the invitations have been sent?"

"Did you call Mr. Rao and tell him that I am to meet him at 12.30 p.m.?"

4. *Impress and insist on results.*

"The eyes of the whole world are on us. We must win."

"Our company must have this business. You can get it. So get that contract."

"I am with you hundred per cent. You have got to finish this before you go home tonight."

"Go after it with every ounce of energy you've got. We must make it by 4.00 p.m. tomorrow."

Conviction is not a technique, but a state of mind to be in. It is a quality, a value, a non-verbal factor which determines our intra-personal as well as inter-personal dealings.

Conviction ensures that the sender means what he says and he believes in it. This state is arrived at only after pondering over the message and arriving at a point of certainty.

Conviction is not a jargon or a cheap trick. It is a way of life.

Conviction does not stand in isolation as an idea to be considered, a technique to be applied, or a trick to be tried. It is an inner state arrived at after much serious consideration.

Yes! When all of us understand the meaning and significance of conviction, we will command people's attention and respect. Our chances of winning would have been made more sure and certain.

How would I rate myself today on the understanding and practice of Conviction?

My score	0	1	2	3	4	5

12

Opportunity and Choice

> "One ship goes East, another goes West,
>   By the self same winds that blow,
> 'Tis the set of sail, and not the gale,
>   That determine the way we go."
>
> "Like the winds of the sea are the waves of Fate,
>   As we voyage along through life,
> 'Tis the set of sail that decides the goal,
>   And not the calm or the strife."

One of the greatest qualities of a successful personality is the ability he/she acquires to recognise the unlimited opportunities that lie all around.

One of the greatest problems, as conceived by many, particularly in India, is the vast population. They call it population explosion. Because of the population explosion, there is a paucity of jobs. And thus there is unemployment. Many are satisfied with blaming the government for not creating sufficient job opportunities.

But this is only true for those who are looking for such *employment*. What about those who are seeking opportunities in the marketplace?

What happened recently in a Productivity Seminar was an eye-opener. The Minister without Portfolio was to inaugurate the proceedings. The guests were requested to be in their seats at 9:25 a.m. The Minister himself came only at 10:20 a.m.

As for speeches, by now I am used to most of them. The Minister was hard-hitting when he said, "*Population problem in our country is at the root of all productivity. If we had less people, we would not have had any more problems. The only solution is less people and more family planning.*" Clap. Clap. Clap. Delegates nodded their heads in agreement.

But, in a Management Seminar a few days later, the same Minister said, "*People are the greatest resource of any nation. All other resources are only secondary. All management is man-power management. All leadership is man-power leadership.*" Again, Clap. Clap. Clap.

Ask any enterprising man, a person with an honourable purpose. To him, more people means more opportunities to make it good in business. He is engaged in fulfilling human needs. The more needs there are, the more successful are these people.

Take a cigarette vendor. Would he like to set up his shop in the midst of a desert?

Take a restaurant owner. He needs people to eat in his establishment. The more, the merrier.

Take a school. They need children to study.

Take a laundry. Take a textile shop. Take a supermarket.

Take any business, any industry, any institution or any service bureau. The population is not a problem for them. It is a valid reason to be working and living. Without people, there will be no enterprise.

Successful people do not find any need to turn an *opportunity* into a *problem* to hoodwink people. Their world is filled with objectives to pursue, with chances to get ahead and with missions to accomplish. They do not find the need to invent excuses to cover up their shortcomings.

- Writing is done through rearranging 26 letters of the alphabet. See the amount of literature and poetry that has been created through using these letters.
- Music is made through seven basic notes.
- Paintings have all come through the seven basic colours.

Where would we have been, if the creative, enterprising people too were content with talking about problems?

But it is also true that sharing the abundance of good that exists in the world is largely a matter of *choice*.

We must understand this *Power of Choice*. Look at the quality of life you are enjoying because you have been born as a human being. Look at the choices you have before you. Look at the many wonderful things human beings have created and are still creating. Look at the many wonderful changes that human beings are able to bring about around them.

In understanding this power of choice, we must also consider the four important characteristics of choice:

1. You can only make the choices, but not the consequences

Early in my life I came to realise that I could only make the choices and could put in as much hard work too. I could plan, I could research, I could provide for the possible pitfalls, and I could perform various actions consciously. But, I could never be absolutely certain that I would gain those final results I desired. Anything could have happened in the meantime. This I had to accept. If I didn't, there would have been no action from my side. And nothing worthwhile could have been accomplished. There would have been only disasters.

Take a farmer. He has to perform so many actions and duties with the hope that things will turn out well for him. There is no guarantee that the rains shall come at the proper time. There is no insurance that the crops shall grow. Here, the farmer trusts Nature and does his work sincerely. And, often, he gets rewarded. For each seed he plants, Nature rewards him with possibly a thousand or more grains.

Take an entrepreneur. He has to take so many calculated risks without any absolute guarantee that he shall succeed. He has to accept those consequences which cannot be guaranteed by anyone. Consequences could be calculated. They could be planned. They could be provided for. *But no one could be absolutely certain about the results.*

Take the case of a businessman.

Take someone who is going for a job interview.

Take anyone who is engaged in the act of fulfilling human needs. They can only make the choices that could lead to success. But they cannot decide on the actual consequences.

2. Your Choices must be Your Own

What really happens to many who do not want to make their own choices but would like to make it on the advice of others? In case they succeed, they shall naturally take the credit. In case they fail, there is always someone available who could be blamed for it. This is a common escape mechanism for not making our own choices.

"What to do? My father told me to study science. That's why I failed."

"What to do? My wife doesn't listen. That's why my children are spoilt."

"What to do? My uncle told me to get into this business. That's why I lost out."

What did YOU want to do? Did you even know? Were you certain about it? Why did you not communicate it to your father, your wife, your children or to that uncle of yours?

Remember, every one of your choices *must be your own.* You could certainly benefit from others, experiences. You could consult them. You could be guided by them. You could even follow them. *But the choices made must be your own.*

3. The Power of Choice is a Talent that must be developed

Human talent is vast. Most people utilise only a small fraction of it. To put the talent to use, it must be developed very carefully.

Every son of a successful businessman does not naturally succeed in the enterprise. The basic talents possibly exist. But they need to be developed. These persons possibly have better opportunities too. In many successful cases, much informal training has been going on from the time of birth.

Is it not true that we see many so-called talented people, lying by the wayside, living as failures?

What really matters is not the amount of talent. *But, the way the available talents were developed and put to proper use.*

4. The Power of Choice is a Special Privilege that YOU as a Human Being are Blessed with

Animals or other living beings do not have this choice available to them.

While conditions remain the same, human beings can choose to live happily or unhappily. They can choose the place for living, the style of living or the thousands of other things that make up life itself. They can choose to be vegetarians or meat-eaters. They can even choose not to make a choice.

Those who shall understand and accept this *Special privilege*, can ensure a more fulfilling quality of life.

How would I rate myself on the understanding and practice of *Opportunity and Choice?*

My Score	0	1	2	3	4	5

13

Success

> *"The achiever is the only person who is truly active. There can be inner satisfaction in simply driving a fine car, eating in a fine restaurant or watching a good movie or television program. Those who think that they're enjoying themselves doing that, are half-dead and don't know it."*
>
> GEORGE ALLEN
> American pro football coach 1974

1887. Francis Younghusband, Captain in the King's Dragoon Guards, stationed in China, was determined to walk from Peking to India across Gobi Desert and Karakoram; a journey of 3,000 miles never before attempted by any man.

With eight camels, a guide, a servant, and a Mongol assistant, he plodded the first 1,000 miles through the interminable desert, mostly at night, before he came to the first house he had seen since starting. From there, it was another 40 days march to Kashgar in Chinese Turdestan, and then south to Yarkand, where he had his first view of the mountains. He had the choice between the easier Karakoram Pass, leading to Leh in Ladakh, or the much higher and virtually unexplored Mustagh Pass into Kashmir. He chose the latter.

As they entered the mountain belt, they were in a pathless country untenanted by man. And on reaching the top of a 15,000-foot pass, the first, they saw ahead of them tiers of peaks—25,000, 26,000 and, in one case, 28,000 feet high. "It was a scene," wrote Younghusband, "which, as I viewed it, and realised that this seemingly impregnable array must be pierced and overcome, seemed to put the iron will into my soul."*

The ascent of the Mustagh Pass was arduous, but they reached the top (19,030) at midday. On the far side, they looked down a steep ice-slope terminating in a precipice several thousand feet high.

"To get down," wrote Younghusband, "seemed to be an impossibility. I had no experience of Alpine climbing, and had no ice-axe or other mountain appliances. I had not even proper boots. All I had for footwear were some native boots of soft leather without nails and without heels . . . which gave me no sort of grip on any icy surface . . . . I kept quiet, silent as I looked over the pass, and waited to hear what the men had to say about it. They meanwhile were looking at me, *and imagining that an Englishman never went back from an enterprise he had once started*, took it as a matter of course that as I gave no order to go back, I meant to go on."

So, they started down the ice-slope. ". . . For six hours we descended the precipice, partly rock and partly ice-slope, and when I reached the bottom and looked back, it seemed impossible that any man could have come down such a slope."

It took the party two more days to traverse the glacier, and a further two to reach Ashkole, the first inhabited spot in India.

Finally, the party arrived in Srinagar. There, the political agent, the first fellow countryman Younghusband had seen in seven months, greeted him with the words, "Don't you think you should have a wash?"

How could Francis Younghusband endure so much agony and loneliness for seven long months on his own choice?

---

* "The Himalayas", *Time/Life Books*, 1975.

WHY INVITE AND ENDURE THE PAIN?

Let us take the case of the legendary hero, Colonel Jim Corbett and his enthralling accounts of hunting man-eaters in the Kumaon hills.*

He wrote, "This was her *four hundred and thirty-sixth human kill*. But this, I think, was the first time she had been followed up so persistently and she now began to show her resentment by growling.

"To appreciate a tiger's growl to the full, it is necessary to be situated as then I was—rocks all around with dense vegetation between—and the imperative necessity of testing each footstep to avoid falling headlong into unseen chasms and caves.

"I cannot expect you, who read this at your fireside, to appreciate my feelings at the time. The sound of growling and the expectation of an attack terrified me at the same time as it gave me hope. If the tigress lost her temper sufficiently to launch an attack, it would give me an opportunity of accomplishing the object for which I had come, by enabling me to get even with her for all the pain and suffering she had caused."

Indeed, for all the sufferings Jim Corbett had to go through, he was rewarded with the result; a job well done.

On another occasion, Jim Corbett wrote: "Cramped, and stiff and hungry—I had been without food for sixty-four hours and with my clothes clinging to me—it had rained for an hour during the night—I descended from the tree when objects were clearly visible...."

For over 15 years, Jim Corbett continued his relentless pursuit of hunting man-eaters. *What made him pursue a purpose which provided him with no comforts, but was filled with dangers at every turn of feet for so many long years? And he was not a hunter by profession.*

You must have heard many more such inspiring tales of people telling us about the pursuit of excellence. Put yourself in their shoes and begin to inquire—What makes them tick as individuals? How could they carry on relentlessly? How does one person succeed where so many before had failed and given up hopes? How and from where do these successful ones manage to get their inspiration?

Is there a single principle that makes all the difference?

---

* *Man-Eaters of Kumaon*, Jim Corbett, Penguin Books.

Is it in action? Do people go on slogging all day feeling certain that they shall be successful?

Is it in the ability to smooth-talk their way through people? Do all those people who have a grand smile, automatically gain fulfilment?

Is it their good fortune in possessing
— a towering personality?
— or a high, formal education?
— or a high I.Q?
— or being supported by an influential godfather?
— or being born in a wealthy family?

While all these could have contributed to the success of many—individually and collectively—it cannot be attributed to a specific characteristic alone.

Definitions of success can be many. But the best I can think of is:

Progressive realisation of
Productive, Useful, Worthwhile and Pre-determined
GOALS
that an individual has set for himself/herself
and shall continue to pursue them,
irrespective of what other people may
Say, Think or Do.

Success is a result of many composite factors. Like a diamond. The presence, and the combination of various factors lead to the formation of carbon into a crystallisation, and the diamond is born. By the variations of those same factors, there exists a range of diamonds from transparent to translucent; some white, some colourless, some yellow, blue or green. Besides these varieties of gems, there are also borts, poorly crystallised or inferior in quality, or in fragmentary condition, or carbonado (black diamond) which vary from gray to black to opaque.

And to discover them, as in the case of gold which we had discussed earlier, we need to engage ourselves in serious prospecting, locating, mining and processing.

The key to any measure of *Success* too lies in systematic processing. Success, like a diamond, has to emerge.

Let us take a closer look at our definition.

Success is related to *GOALS*.

Only *My Goals* can tell me if I am successful. Do I know my Goals? Goals are that essential as the measuring-point for

Success. Without knowing it, how can I, or anyone else, say I was successful or not?

Do I know My Goals? Have I thought about them, and planned to work for attaining them? Do I know what I want to accomplish in the short-range as well as the long-range areas of my life? Have I consciously or unconsciously, formally or informally planned for them?

Now, the *Progressive realisation*.

Nothing is accomplished in a jiffy; just like that. It takes time and efforts. The results come progressively. The realisation too. For this, a person should become aware of his goals; long-term as well as short-term. And, then the actions and the work geared towards attaining them are initiated and goals accomplished.

But these must also pass a four-way test:

Is this realisation *Productive?*
> Was that ration between the *Time and the Efforts* (input) and the *Results* (output) gained in my favour?

Is this realisation *Useful?*
> Can I use the gains from it, in some or other areas of my life?

Is this realisation *Worthwhile?*
> Was it worth all the Time and Efforts that I put into attaining the goal?

Is this realisation *Predetermined?*
> Does all that is gained, form an integral part of a clear goal that was determined beforehand?

Now, that which the *individual has set for himself/herself.*

Have I set those goals myself, and am I happy about having set them?

And, *continues to pursue them irrespective of what others may say, think, or do.*

And, will the outcome from all these be acceptable to me as a part of my success?

Further, *Success is related to potentials and goals.*

Does financial success mean having lots of money to throw around?

The Chairman of the Board was congratulating the new M.D. In his speech he said, "Ladies and Gentlemen. This young man here has risen to the position of the Chief Executive within a short span of three years. Let us now congratulate him." Clap.

Clap. Clap. "Now, let us also request our new Chief to speak a few words to us."

Thereby, the new Chief stands up and says, "Thank you, Daddy, for all the wonderful things you said about me." Is this what financial success is, or for that matter, being successful at all? No. Certainly not.

Financial success is a rate of exchange of effectiveness. It is not the result of earning money. *Earning money is the result of financial success.*

Career success is not the result of earning promotions. *Growth, promotions and fulfillment of goals are the results of career success.*

Social success is not the result of earning positions. *Deserving social positions and attaining them thus is social success.*

Many individuals have discovered that though they have great wealth, they are not successful if they are intellectually sterile, spiritually barren, socially rejected, emotionally unstable, physically broken or rejected by their families.

Success is a journey and not a destination.

Really successful people have understood *success* to be more than acquiring money, property and the products that money can buy.

Some find it in their work.
Some find it in the journey itself.
Some find it in the high standards of excellence in the tune with the values they live by.

And . . . different people have different measures

Carl Duerr has an international reputation for putting ailing companies on the road to stable profitability. One of his best known successes was the 1968-70 rescue operation of the UK Jenson Motors Ltd. Others include the reorganisation of Europe's largest retail jewellery store chain, making profits during the eight years of the operation of an Industrial equipment-maker, and raising the production and sales of a German knitting mill by 600 per cent.

In his book, *Management Kinetics,* Carl Duerr writes about the industrial equipment manufacturer:

> Maybe the Dean wanted to be shot of me. Anyhow, his recommendation landed me the job of Chief Engineer and

Production Manager. At 25 or so I chucked sales engineering, threw over teaching, and went for management hammer and tongs. I put in twelve-to-fifteen-hour days, did a lot of things wrong but enough right so that the company graduated from a net worth of minus $15,000 to a point three years later where the old man sold out for $3 million. The erstwhile wheelbarrow maker now is a very well-known machine tool company.

Carl Duerr is one of those people whom we call 'trouble shooters'. Within his own sphere, he had learned the combination that makes winning possible.

Describing this aspect of personality, Carl Duerr quotes Rudyard Kipling:

"*But a fool must follow his natural bent (even as you and I!)*"

The operative word here is *natural*.

How would I rate myself on my understanding of *Success* today?

My Score	0	1	2	3	4	5

14

Self-image

> "Man is a singular creature. He has a set of gifts which make him unique among the animals, so that unlike them he is not a figure in the landscape—he is the shaper of the landscape."
>
> JACOB BRONOWSKI
> British scientist

It is important that we should understand more about this concept of Self-image and how it affects the way we turn out to be. The truth is that we are always influenced and governed by the Self-image.

Your *Self-image* reflects the overall attitudes you hold; unified, crystallised, set of propositions which you have formed towards your capabilities in a multitude of areas. It is the picture you have created about yourself, and something which you hold firm

Self-image is the ceiling you have imposed on the effectiveness with which you can use your *true potentials*.

SELF-IMAGE CHECK

On the following pages, you will find a checklist describing areas of your self-image. They are also explained.

Fill in the 'Assets *Today* Column,' giving yourself a rating ranging from 0 to 100. You will have opportunities to check this again after six months.

Move quickly through each item. Do not spend too much time thinking and deciding about each item. Write down the first number that comes to your consciousness. Your subconscious mind will provide you with the answer as you begin the list.

There are no right or wrong answers here. It is your view that you hold about yourself today that matters.

This is strictly for your private assessment only. It need not be shown to anyone else.

	Self-Image Check		
	ASSETS Degree to which you consider yourself positive about this specific trait. Maximum points 100		
		Today	After 6 months
1. **Self acceptance.** (I like myself the way I am as of today.)		_____	_____
2. **My ability and the presence of mind to speak the right thing.** (I know that I can depend upon my inner self to guide me to behave and act in the most appropriate manner whenever needed.)		_____	_____
3. **Competence on the job.** (I am able to perform all those jobs which I am responsible for in a most competent, efficient and productive manner.)		_____	_____

Self-image

	Today	After 6 months

4. **Enjoy meeting people.** (I do enjoy meeting and interacting with people; whether known or unknown to me.) _____ _____

5. **Competence in managing my time.** (I generally do not have to offer excuses like, 'I did not have the time', to finish those jobs which I am responsible for. I generally do all my jobs within the time limits allotted to me/by me.) _____ _____

6. **Enjoy doing the work.** (Generally, I am happy being engaged in the work that I am to perform. I really do enjoy the work that I am responsible enough to perform.) _____ _____

7. **Engaged in continual self-development.** (Generally, I am always learning about ways and means of making myself a better and competent person. For this purpose, I read, I listen, I discuss, I attend training seminars and am always alert.) _____ _____

8. **I know what is good for me and I can generally assert myself.** (I can generally speak about my beliefs without feelings of guilt and intentions to cause any hurt to others. I also know how to stand up for my rights without involving myself in fights and guilt. Although I am very firm, I generally do not hurt others intentionally.) _____ _____

9. **I generally remain cheerful.** (I do believe that life is to be enjoyed irrespective of the conditions around me. I find many wonderful things around me and I am happy about them.) _____ _____

	Today	After 6 months
10. **Enjoy being close to nature.** (I feel wonderful when I am with the nature and its elements. I love the trees, mountains, rivers, picnics, camping and the outdoors.)		
11. **Ability to create trust in others.** (Generally, people do tend to believe and trust me. I too feel I am worthy of trust because of the way I think and deal with people in general. I do deserve to be trusted by others.)		
12. **Capacity to earn money.** (I know that money is a necessity and am capable of earning it whenever I need it. I also understand the value of money and generally know how to put them to proper uses.)		
13. **Capacity to imagine new possibilities and alternatives.** (I generally do not get stuck in doing things only in certain fixed ways. I generally can think of many alternate ways. I am open to suggestions and willing to experiment.)		
14. **Courage to change and form habits.** (I realise the importance of being in charge of my habits. I am not a slave of my habits. I have the courage to experiment, change and create new habits that shall help me towards more fulfilment.)		
15. **Self-reliance.** (Generally, I do not tend to blame others for my failures. I know I can depend on my talents and my mind to see me through when problems arise. I do place more reliability within me than on others.)		

Self-image

	Today	After 6 months

16. Maintaining a healthy family relationship. (I love my family and I am very happy being with them. Generally, there are no serious conflicts within my family because of me. I feel happy to maintain a healthy family relationship.) _____ _____

17. Controlling my behaviour. (I know how I am generally behaving. I do have good control over myself. I am not easily carried away by what others may say, think or do.) _____ _____

18. In touch with my feelings. (I do generally know what I feel. I do know generally how others feel too. I have no difficulties in accepting my feelings. I am considerate of others' feelings too.) _____ _____

19. Self-confidence. (I generally feel very confident about my ability to face the world and act appropriately. I do know that 'I can'. I do depend on myself and my abilities. I generally do not blame others for my difficulties and my failures.) _____ _____

20. Capacity to relax. (I generally do not create unwanted tensions within me, or around me. When I face difficulties, I think in a relaxed manner and find practical ways of solving problems. I do remain cool, collected and serene. I also know practical ways to remain relaxed and comfortable.) _____ _____

Now add up the total and divide it by 20. _____ _____

My Self-image score is : _____ _____

15
Conditioning

> "To be nobody but yourself, in a world which is doing its best, night and day to make you into everybody else—means to fight the hardest battle which any human being can fight; and never stop fighting."
>
> E.E. CUMMINGS
> American poet

Each one of us is born free, special, full of spontaneity, creativity and with a readiness to learn. Full of life and eagerness to learn new things, we learn a great deal during the initial years. We want to touch everything, feel, taste, smell, hear and want to experience the variety and richness of life. Curiosity is highest during those years as a toddler. And, we learn the maximum during these years too.

But what happens to those special gifts during the process of growing into adulthood?

FAMILY INFLUENCE

Almost from the moment of birth, each one of us has been conditioned by the influences that surround us. *Family, Friends, Society, Institutions*—virtually everything we came in contact with have influenced us.

We are conditioned by 'influence' rather than by some deliberate attempts to mould us. *Father, Mother, Brothers, Sisters, Uncles, Relatives*—all have influenced us, particularly so during our childhood.

By examples, by words, advice, arguments, or persuasion, our families gave us ideas of what to expect of ourselves. And, unfortunately, some of those ideas were very limited in their scope.

Let us take the case of food habits of people all over. They differ in so many ways and I am not speaking merely about the 'tastes'. Some eat meat and others don't. Broadly, people are termed as vegetarians and non-vegetarians.

Among the vegetarians themselves, there are so many differences. In India, there are some who consider fish to be vegetarian and enjoy eating it. Then there are other vegetarians who would not even touch onions, potatoes and those vegetables which grow under the ground.

Among those who are non-vegetarians, the less said, the better. There are those who relish eating meat, but shall not even touch beef or pork. There are beef-eaters for whom even thinking of eating pork is a sin. Leave alone those who shall not even hesitate to eat a horse, frog and even snake.

The very discussion of this topic could have a revolting, nauseating effect on some of us. Isn't it all a matter of conditioning? All of us are used to behaving in certain set ways. In due course, we even consider our set ways as sacrosanct and immutable. Anything that is seen differently from what we have been used to, is even considered as something to be abhorred and rejected. Aren't all these purely personal and due to conditioning?

Let us take religion as another example. Religion truly is a path to find the divine. It is also true that every religion tells us that God is one for all. If so, why are there so many quarrels and divisions in the name of religion all over the world? Why was there and still is so much killing, hatred and bloodshed? Why is there so much intolerance? Are all these really religious? Yet, why do most stick to those set ways and even consider the ways of others as wrong and sinful? See the effects of conditioning?

Every social system is engaged in conditioning its members to think, believe and behave in set ways. And, most of them even come to think of those ways practised by others as wrong, going even to the extent of condemning them. There are fights and even wars based on this kind of conditioning. Why should there be any fights because someone chooses to behave in ways that are different from those I have adopted? See the effects of conditioning everywhere?

Our family influences work on us either as a positive or negative type of conditioning.

Why do we tend to walk only on the footpaths set out on the roads? By conditioning we know that they help to protect us.

Why do we drive our cars and vehicles on the paths already determined by the society?

Why do we earnestly follow so many set rules and regulations?

All conditioning is not bad or negative. But, certainly there are many set ways that bring about many unwanted limitations without our being even aware of them? Sometimes, we may even become aware of them, yet, we do not take any initiatives to make even an iota of change in them. That is conditioning for you, and for me.

We are certainly not condemning all conditioning as bad or as undesirable. We are only saying that they are an essential part of life. But, all of us need to become aware of the behaviour based on conditioning.

Luckily, for those who are committed to develop a winning personality, except for extreme traumatic experiences of early childhood, most negative conditioning of childhood can be easily overcome.

ENVIRONMENT AND INSTITUTIONS

There are so many outside agencies too that exert a considerable influence on the individual personality. In school the teacher, other students and those who become our friends, influence and condition us. In the neighborhood, those people that we frequently interact with, do affect us. Scenes change, names change; but the influences continue to bombard our behaviour.

Certainly, all influences are not bad. There is much that is good. *But, retaining our true identity and developing our innate potential becomes the real challenge while growing into full bloom.*

This is a battle which we have to continue fighting and not stop fighting ever.

CHECK THE EFFECT OF YOUR CONDITIONING

Are you conditioned to think and act too rigidly?
Do you still possess the flexibility necessary to get the joy out of living?

Try to solve the following:

1. A little girl put a small coin (25 paise) in an empty wine bottle, closed the bottle with a cork and challenged me to remove the coin *without breaking the bottle or taking the cork out.*

    I tried various methods for about 15 minutes and could not achieve the feat.

    When I gave up, she took the bottle and solved the problem in a few seconds. How did she do it?

2. If I can build a square wall around one acre plot of land at a certain height with 12 truckloads of bricks, how big a square plot can I enclose with a similarly high wall with 24 truckloads of bricks?

3. Mark the *colour/shade/tint* that is concealed in each of the following sentences.

    Each of the sentences contains a different colour. The same colour is not repeated twice.

    The challenge to you is to ensure that you complete the whole game within *10 minutes*. See if you can achieve it within the time limit.

Examples

—Freelance journalists then undertook *newspaper editing* work at a faster pace. (red)

—Then they observed that the *mob lacked* proper leadership. (black)

Now complete the test:
1. After a long peg, Reynolds began to dance faster.
2. To the priest, and the cop, persuasion came naturally.
3. When you let an idiot guide you, you go astray.
4. As he let out the loud yell, owls flew away from the tree.
5. Fools scratch the brow, nip the bud and eat hurriedly.
6. Then there was Jog, older than Sharma, who was very good at singing.
7. Both Charan and his car let out a growl when the gas level is high.
8. With minimum food and meagre entertainment, what else can you expect from them?
9. From then on, every new tax law hit entertainment industry very adversely.
10. On Sunday mornings, he has to tuck the overall in, dig out weeds and water the gardens.
11. Though an accomplished academician, Patiram Mali lacked a sense of humour.
12. Investigations showed that in Ghata tehsil, very many farmers had become rich.
13. Even the water tap, in keeping in tune with other utilities, went out of order.
14. The rule stated that Apple growing inside, Pear lying outside, should not be collected.
15. He was glad that at least he could watch Rome through the windows.
16. At the sight of his love, Lobo ran gently towards her.
17. Paulo and Lolo lived at the far end of the street.
18. No one thought of awnings to protect the wheat from the rains.
19. Whatever else may not be true, but the richest nuts came from the valley of Bhonda.
20. Why should the Slav end errands?
21. Now with the certificate in hand, Narinder Boch resumed his practice as a medical professional.

4. Can you discover a sensible link between the word 'ALTERNOSIPY' and the following words?

Assertive	Enthusiastic	Immaculate	Lofty
Natural	Observant	Poised	Refined
Skilful	Tenacious	Youthful	

Answers to 'Check the Effect Of Your Conditioning' on pages 89-91.

1. She pushed the cork inside. 2. 4 acres. 3.1 grey
3.2 copper 3.3 tan 3.4 yellow 3.5 brown
3.6 gold 3.7 scarlet 3.8 green 3.9 white
3.10 indigo 3.11 lilac 3.12 silver 3.13 pink
3.14 pearly 3.15 chrome 3.16 orange 3.17 olive
3.18 fawn 3.19 chestnut 3.20 lavender 3.21 ochre

4. An obvious answer most people shall come up with will be "The first letters of all the words put together shall make the word ALTERNOSIPY."

But a better answer will be "If all the letters of ALTERNOSIPY are rearranged, it shall read PERSONALITY and the words given are attributes of a personality."

16

Your Beliefs Affect Your Style of Functioning

> "Injustice, poverty, slavery, ignorance—these may be cured by reform or revolution. But men do not live only fighting evils. They live by positive goals, individual and collective, a vast variety of them, seldom predictable, at times incompatible."
>
> SIR ISAIAH BERLIN
> British philosopher

Behind every decision you make and every action you take, there are beliefs about human nature and human behaviour. Many of these beliefs are formulated in early childhood as a part of our conditioning.

Your Beliefs Affect Your Style of Functioning

A significant aspect of this conditioning process is the development of the *self-concept*. Your self-concept includes your ideas on how you should play your roles in various situations that you come across during day-to-day living.

As an example, let us consider the case of Mona.

Mona is the only daughter of her proud and dominating mother. Her father, a simple, quiet man, has taken a position in the home as a silent spectator and a 'Yes Man' to his wife. You would hardly ever see him expressing an opinion in front of his wife.

Mona's mother always claimed that her daughter was the most beautiful girl in the whole world. But she never gave Mona any chance whatsoever to express her own feelings. Mona had to always sing in tune with what her mother said.

Years rolled on. Mona grew up and today she is a wife, married to a smart, educated, young man. And, she was truly happy in the company of her loving husband, Robert. They both lived happily in their own home in Chembur, which was about four miles away from her mother's home at Mahim.

But the mother has not truly accepted the fact that Mona is now a lady in her own right, running her own household. Let us see what happens between these two.

As the Friday morning comes up, Mona receives a call from her mother: "Darling. Please come over to Mahim. You and Robert shall spend the weekend with us."

Mona wants to say no; but she doesn't have the courage to say so. Robert had even begun to express his unhappiness at having to spend the weekends with Mona's mother. But, being in love with Mona, he could only grunt and grumble indirectly. He has been tolerating the situation. Therefore, even though reluctantly, Mona would obey her mother. And, after reaching her mother's home, she would be forced to phone Robert in his office and ask him to come to her mother's place for the weekend.

Whenever Mona raises some excuses for not coming over, her mother overrides her and Mona is so deftly manipulated that she has to say 'Yes' to her mother's demands.

The major barrier in Mona today is the belief, "I should not say anything that will make my mother dislike me." There was this overly strong belief that under no circumstances should she ever express any feeling which her mother may disapprove of. Mona's relationship with her husband was causing unwanted strains. And, Mona had no idea whatsoever how to handle this situation. She could only plead with her husband to understand and to keep tolerating her mother.

Mona's beliefs and behaviour had been formulated when she was a little girl. Her behaviour was reinforced for sidestepping conflicts and not ruffling anyone's feathers, specifically so of her mother. She had only learned to be friendly and obliging. This is where the troubles began.

Mona's role in the system has now changed. She is a wife. Thus, instead of avoiding personal conflicts, she is expected to confront and solve them. Instead of dodging controversial decisions, she has to find ways to face up to them. Whereas previously the system was manipulated to make Mona into a "mother-pleaser", she was now held responsible enough to do things not merely to please others, but to be a good wife.

The result was an unhappy wife and an equally unhappy husband torn apart with feelings of guilt, anger, and frustration.

Let us structure this a little more carefully for a better understanding.

The problem starts with *Beliefs and Viewpoints*.

The specific factors that have contributed to these beliefs and viewpoints were:

1. *One's Self-image as one sees one's self, as one desires to be.*
2. *Perceptions; experience of reality—real and/or distorted.*
3. *Ego needs.*
4. *One's impulses; basic urges.*
5. *Images one has about the family, society, mission and needs.*
6. *Reactions to conflict situations.*
7. *One's past experiences.*

Now, the effects of Conditioning:

Interpretations.	Motto.
Obligations.	Attitudes.
Need for love and respect.	Rules of the family.
Morals; should's and must's.	Habits/Customs.
Need for social acceptance.	Prejudices.

Your Beliefs Affect Your Style of Functioning

Resulting Actions

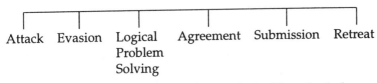

Attack   Evasion   Logical   Agreement   Submission   Retreat
                   Problem
                   Solving

As we can clearly see from this analysis, Mona had chosen the extreme step of *Retreat* into her shell and in the process remained suffering.

In contrast to this, the answer certainly is not the other extreme step of *Attack* either. That could dehumanise Mona and bring more suffering to herself and to the people whom she loves.

The retreat step is what is generally known as being *Passive*. The attack step is what is known as being *Aggressive*. Either of these is not the answer. The essential need is to arrive at a 'Logical Problem Solving' approach and this is what, for the want of a better word, is meant by the term 'being *Assertive*'.

Unless understood properly, **assertive** is generally thought of more in the shades of being **aggressive**. Being *aggressive* and being *assertive* are two *different approaches*. Thus, a clearer explanation of being *Assertive* could be considered as being *Gentle and Strong*. That's it; being gentle and strong at the same time, *without any feelings of guilt and without any intentions to cause any hurt to others.*

Let us see what happens when Mona becomes Gentle and Strong towards her mother; when she becomes *Assertive*.

Another Friday morning, the phone rings and Mona picks it up.

"Mona darling, this is your Mother. Come over to Mahim. You may spend the weekend with us."

By now Mona has been trained to be *assertive*.

She replies: "Mummy, I wish I could come. But, I don't think I will be able to make it."

"What do you mean, you won't be able to make it? *Don't you love your mother anymore?*"

"Mummy dear, I love you. But Robert has told me that he has another weekend programme. So, I won't be able to make it."

"You can't speak to your mother like this. What will happen to all the vegetables I have bought for you two?"

"Yes, mummy. What will happen to the vegetables? But I love you, mummy. All I said was that I won't be able to make it this weekend."

"You can't speak to me like this. After all, I am your mother."

"I love you, mummy dear. All I said was that I won't be able to make it this weekend."

"But children shouldn't speak to their mother like this. What is happening to this world?"

"I love you, mummy dear. All I said was we won't be able to come this weekend."

"In that case, you should have phoned me and told me earlier. Now what will happen to all the vegetables I have bought for you?"

"Yes, mummy. What will happen to all the vegetables? All I said was that I won't be able to make it this weekend. I wish I could have informed you earlier. Robert told me only last night about this programme."

"Now, now. You can't speak to me like this. This means you don't love me anymore."

"Mummy, dear. I love you dearly. All I said was that we won't be able to make it this weekend."

"No, no. I don't want to hear all these silly excuses. Speak to your father." With these words, the mother is giving up her efforts and forcing the father to take up the cudgel on her behalf.

If you do understand this story so far, you will possibly know that the father is secretly feeling happy for his daughter.

He takes up the phone and says:

"Yes, darling. What is the matter. Your mummy is weeping."

"Daddy! Is mummy weeping? All I said was that we won't be able to come over this weekend. Robert has some other plans."

"I see. Then why is mummy crying?"

"I really do not know, daddy. All I said was that I won't be able to come over this weekend."

"Are you sure, darling?"

"Yes, daddy. Tell mummy that I love her more than ever."

"OK. OK. Speak to your mummy." And, he hands over the phone back. Secretly he is happy that his daughter has learned to be assertive now.

Now, the only alternative left for the mother is to arrive at a *Workable Compromise*. All her clever manipulations are not working on her daughter anymore. If anyone has to, it is the

Your Beliefs Affect Your Style of Functioning

mother who must save her face now. So, it goes:

"Darling, in that case, will you come over next weekend?"

"I do wish I could mummy, dear. I will talk to Robert and phone you next Friday."

"Please try to adjust your programme. After all, I am your mother. I will expect you here next Friday."

"Mummy, I love you dearly. I will talk to Robert and inform you by next Friday."

"Please try, and don't forget."

"Yes, mummy."

Now, as the mother puts down the telephone, her reactions could be to heave a sigh and say, "Now, I can die peacefully. My daughter has grown up and she can take care of herself."

If you carefully study the exchange between Mona and her mother, after she learned to be more *assertive*, you will notice certain basic, positive changes in her behaviour style:

— She learned ways to stick to the point in a discussion without becoming angry or anxious.
— She learned to work with others in a spirit of cooperation and mutual respect.
— She learned to confront problems effectively, instead of putting them off.
— She acquired respect from others while building her own self-confidence.

17

Response Styles: Aggressive, Assertive, Passive

> "Reality is a staircase going neither up nor down. We don't move, today is today, always today."
>
> OCTAVIO PAZ
> Mexican poet

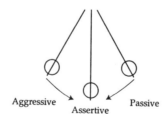

The pendulum of a clock is busy swinging throughout the day, throughout the week, the month and for years. "Why does the pendulum swing? What does it want? What would its reply be to our question, if only it could speak?"

Response Styles

Think for a moment. Why does the pendulum of a clock keep swinging?

The truth is that it cannot stop because others have wound it and pushed it.

But the answer of the pendulum, if it had the capacity to speak at all, shall be, *"Whenever I am made to swing, I am constantly praying that I shall come to a stop, and that too, at the centre."*

"If what you want is to stop, then why don't you?"

"I can't. Others have wound me and are pushing me. Everything I do is to come to the centre and stop. But, I am unable to achieve it."

The pendulum wants to stop at the centre. However, when it is able to stop, and, that too, for a mere fraction of a second, is only at the two extreme ends. And, the speed of the swing is maximum at the centre point; the position where it really wants to stop.

This is the paradox. Like that pendulum, people are often wound and pushed around by others. They want to find the centre and remain there. But, they are unable to achieve it. They do not know how to do it.

But, life is not in the extremes. It is always in the middle.

The pathway is not either at the left end or the right end. These are merely the limits. They are mere parameters. The path itself is *in the middle.*

Being centred means having the ability to recover one's balance, even in the midst of action. A centred person is not subject to passing whims or sudden excitement.

Being grounded, being centred, means being down-to-earth, having gravity or weight. *I know where I stand, and I know what I stand for: that is the ground."*

THE CENTRED BEHAVIOUR

Let us take a moment to check your understanding of the behaviour that is centred. After reading the following situations, classify each response according to whether you think it to be *aggressive, assertive* or *passive.*

1. Kumar, employed as a stenographer in a business enterprise, has been doing his job exceptionally well. When he was appointed, his boss had told him that the Company would consider some attractive increase in Kumar's salary after one

year if he was found to be competent and satisfactory to the management.

After one year, when he discussed this matter with his boss, he was told that the Company cannot afford it now and that Kumar must wait for another six months. Kumar responds:

    A. "O.K. I will check with you after six months." _____

    B. "I believe that the increase I am requesting is reasonable, and you agree that my responsibilities have increased. I would like to discuss this matter further." _____

    C. "I was promised this increment. I deserve it, and I want it now." _____

2. Dinesh is among a group of friends who travel together in the local train to work and back. He is often asked by others to do 'run errand' jobs. There is a news item that the excess amount collected as stamp duty is being refunded. Dinesh is being asked by his colleagues to go to the taluq office and collect the forms for all. Dinesh responds:

    A. "Sure. I will do it." _____

    B. "I would like to let someone else take his turn today. If you would recall, I went to the CIDCO office last time." _____

    C. "I don't like you people pushing me around. Just because I am quiet, it doesn't mean that I am a servant." _____

3. Rakesh is coordinating a project with a colleague for a forthcoming funds collection drive. But, he is doing all the work himself. He says:

    A. "You are not doing your part of the work. If I don't get some cooperation from you, I am going to report to the Programme Chairman." _____

    B. "On paper, we are coordinating this project. Yet, I see that I am doing all the work myself. I would like to talk with you about changing this." _____

    C. Nothing. Rakesh continues to do all the work himself by staying late. _____

Response Styles

4. Ganesh is a Purchase Clerk attached to Department A. A manager from Department B needs some specific work to be done in the market. Instead of doing it himself, the manager asks Ganesh to get them done during his next trip. Ganesh is already hard pressed to complete certain deadlines given to him by his immediate boss. He says:

   A. "I just can't get these materials for you right now. I might be able to get them for you next week. Would it be O.K.?" _____

   B. "You should not be asking me to do this job. I am already pressed for time to finish my tasks. So I won't be able to get them for you." _____

   C. At present I am finding it difficult to complete my deadlines. I prefer not to add on additional work unless it is very essential. Tell me more about your problem and maybe we could think of some alternative." _____

5. Anu has a son who neither studies properly nor takes his responsibilities seriously. She has talked about this to her son on many occasions. Today, she says:

   A. "It looks to me as if you are just careless and irresponsible. Or maybe you just don't have the intelligence to do your work properly." _____

   B. "You know it is my job as your mother to see that you study properly and everything goes on well. I hope this doesn't upset you. I want to help you as much as I can. I don't see any reason why we cannot cooperate with each other properly." _____

   C. "We have talked about your studies and your goals in life. But the results are not up to the levels we had agreed upon. I want you to improve your performance. Now, let us discuss what you are going to do in the future." _____

THE AGGRESSIVE STYLE

Aggressive people often express their feelings at the expense of others. They have the attitude, *"I have the rights, others don't. What you want is less important than what I want."*

Mona's mother was a good example of an aggressive personality. Look at some of the statements she made:

"Come over to Mahim. You may spend the weekend with us." (An order)

"Don't you love your mother anymore?" (An accusation)

"What will happen to the vegetables I have bought for you two?" (Another accusation)

"You can't speak to me like this. I am your mother." (One more accusation)

"In that case, you should have phoned me and told me earlier." (You are guilty)

Aggressive people create a double bind for themselves:

1. *They do not respect anyone they can dominate.*
2. *They are afraid of an equal relationship.*

Each of us have an inborn need to love people and use things. An aggressive individual has turned this around:

He or she *uses people* and *loves things*.

Excessive use of the aggressive style often perpetuates the 'passive aggressive'/'hidden aggressive' mode of behaviour.

The Passive Aggressive/Hidden Aggressive Style

Example: The subordinate of an aggressive boss reports absent when he/she is really needed in the office.

It is a defence mechanism that people develop for survival in an environment where they feel helpless and powerless.

THE PASSIVE STYLE

Most often the passive behaviour results from and results in *feelings of fear, anxiety, guilt,* and *physical and emotional stress*.

Passive individuals tend to feel that outside forces are controlling them; they have low self-esteem and a negative self-image.

Excessively passive behaviour leads to a non-cooperative response from others.

Mona's behaviour, before she learned to be assertive, is a perfect example.

Response Styles

THE ASSERTIVE STYLE

The assertive style is based on our natural rights as human beings:

To be treated with respect, to be ourselves, to have and to live in tune with our values.

Each of us has a unique personal space which must be respected by those with whom we interact. As we move outside our space into the common area where others are, we must respect the rights of others too.

Those statements made by Mona after she learned to be assertive may be checked as examples:

"Mummy, dear. I love you dearly. All I said was that we won't be able to make it this weekend."

Another important element of the assertive style is the responsibility—*responsibility for oneself, not others!* This means setting limits to take care of yourself while accepting the consequences of your actions. You state what you want without violating the rights of others.

You and I have many rights to lead our lives meaningfully and purposefully. Often, we are not aware of the ways of expressing our rights properly and effectively. This is the major cause that leads us to remain either as *Aggressive or Passive*.

As human beings we do have many natural rights. Most of us have not learned them, nor have we learned to apply them practically in our day-to-day living.

But, knowing them and applying them shall make a considerable difference in the way we develop our personalities. To understand these aspects more, let us take a closer look at some of our basic *rights* and *responsibilities*. Remember, the *rights* and *responsibilities* always go hand-in-hand. Every time I shall express a right, I have to accept the responsibility that it shall bring about too. It is extremely important that you and I shall always remember both of these characteristics.

Responses to Quiz on pages 100–101:
1B, 2B, 3B, 4C and 5C are assertive responses.
1C, 2C, 3A, 4B and 5A are aggressive responses.
1A, 2A, 3C, 4A and 5B are passive responses.

18

My Assertive Human Rights

> *"Any tradition which has been established for a long time must be compatible with basic needs of human nature."*
> —JOHN BENSON
> British academic

1. **I have the right to take responsibility for the initiation of my behaviour, thoughts and emotions, and handle the consequences they may create**
   When someone tells me, 'You can't behave like that', 'You can't think like that,' or You can't feel like that,' the truth is still "I am behaving like that," "I do think like that," and "I do feel that way." If I am willing to accept the consequences they may create, then where is the difficulty? If I have *no intentions to cause any hurt to others* and *if I am gentle and strong about my behaviour*, then where is the problem? Under these conditions, I shall never hurt anyone intentionally. I am, after all, accepting the responsibility.
   One of the basic problems with most of us is that we behave, think and emote in certain special ways. But, we are not willing

to take the responsibilities that go with it, nor do we want to handle the consequences our behaviour may create. Once this is understood properly and applied, you too can become more assertive, and benefit from it. No one will be able to manipulate you unless you are willing to adjust that way.

2. **I have the right to state my limits, expectations, and feelings about other people's behaviour in a manner that respects their self-esteem**

Someone (a friend or a close relative) asks me for a loan of money. In the past, this person had never returned the loans within a reasonable time. I do not want to grant him that request now. Can I not say so? Do I know how to say it without hurting the other person's self-esteem? We agree that it is difficult to do so. But, it can be and must be done. It certainly can be learned and applied too.

Let us say, I told him, *"I won't be able to give you that loan."* If the other person truly loves me, he must simply accept my statement. But does he/she do it that way? In reality, they try various techniques to make me feel guilty and act in ways that suit their conveniences. Often they find it easy to make me feel guilty and manipulate me in the process.

"Why can't you give me a loan? It means you don't love me anymore." The other person is doing *guilt manipulation* on me by suggesting that I do not love him anymore. All because he wants me to behave in a manner that suits him. Without realising this, most people generally get caught up within these manipulations and suffer in the name of friendship. Do I not have a right to set my limits? After all, I have no intentions to hurt the other person.

So, I shall continue to speak *gently and strongly, without any intentions to hurt the other person and without any feelings of guilt within me*, by replying, "I do understand what you are asking. But, I won't be able to give you that loan."

Do I have to always answer the 'why'? If I choose to offer an explanation, it need be done only to someone who truly cares for my feelings and is willing to listen to and understand me.

3. **I have the right to decide if I am responsible for solving other people's problems and to help them to solve their own problems.**

Anu's son, as we had seen earlier, did not do his homework properly. Does Anu not have the right and the responsibility to insist on ways to change her son's behaviour? What happens when Anu does not know how to be assertive? The child shall continue *to manipulate his mother in the name of love and remain irresponsible towards his studies. He would even make it appear that his studies is the responsibility of his mother.* Many of them do so. Why should it be that way?

Therefore, Anu replies to him, "We have talked several times about your studies and your goals in life. But the results are not up to the levels we had agreed upon. I want you to improve your performance. Now, let us discuss what you are going to do in the future." Now, Anu is being assertive.

4. I have the right to change my mind

Last night, during a cocktail party, one of the guests asked you to grant him a favour. You were less defensive under the influence of liquor. Normally, you would have said 'no.' Thus, the other person had waited for a suitable opportunity when you were less defensive and then trapped you with a 'yes' reply.

Today, as you began thinking about your promise, you realized that the other person had trapped you last night. Do you not have the right to change your mind?

Of course, you have that right. But what happens when you tell him so. He will use so many manipulations to make you feel guilty and make you accept that you are breaking a solemn promise. Are you really doing so? What shall happen if you will tell him gently and strongly, *"I have changed my mind."* You have no intentions to hurt him. You are not guilty at all for changing your mind.

If you shall remain assertive now, the chances are that there will be less attempts by the other person to manipulate you further. Even the friendship between you shall grow stronger. You will be much happier in the long run.

5. I have the right to make mistakes, to be responsible for them, and to learn from them

So many people were waiting around me (there are many even today) ready to jump on me, and say, "You can't make a mistake like that." They appeared happy that I had made a mistake so that they could shout at me with an 'I-told-you-so attitude' and manipulate me to suit their needs.

"What do you mean I *can't* make a mistake like that? I did. That's a fact. I accept it and I am responsible for it too."

"To err is human," they say. If so, why do you take delight in rubbing my mistakes on me, and ensure that I am made to feel

My Assertive Human Rights

guilty about it? *Do you ever tell me what I should do in the future to ensure that such errors are not made?*

"I do not make errors intentionally. It happens. It happened. Now if you do care for me, you will teach me how to avoid them in future. You will also teach me to be responsible for my mistakes. You don't ever seem to understand this truth. Now, whether *you understand it or not*, on my part *I am responsible for my mistakes and I shall learn from them too.* Certainly, I am not going to allow you to manipulate me just because I made a mistake."

6. I have the right to say, "I don't know"

Being a teacher myself, my students do ask me many questions. Sometimes, I do not know the right answer. What should I do? Bluff them? Cheat them? Am I supposed to be having all the answers ready with me always?

If I bluff them now, it would only make me a master bluffer in the long run. Why can't I honestly say, "I do not know the answer now."

Personally speaking, I have always found that my students felt good, and respected me more, whenever I did say, "I don't know." However, from that moment on, my whole personality will seriously begin the search for the correct answer. Invariably, before I met those students again, I would discover the answer too. I became wiser in the process. The understanding and trust between me and my students grew. *We felt good in that process of learning from each other.*

It is only that person who can honestly say, "I don't know" (when he did not know) who can ever learn anything new. More understanding will come to such a person because he has an open mind. Even more important, specifically so within the context we are referring to, *it is only that person who can honestly say, "I don't know" who can learn anything new.*

Look at the benefits you shall gain by being able to say, "I don't know." You will have no guilt. Others will not be able to manipulate you. You will learn more. And, you will continue to grow wiser.

When you do not know a thing, say so assertively.

7. I have the right to be treated with respect

People, specifically the younger lot, find joy in pulling others' legs. Quite often, they go beyond the limits and even find joy in hurting the other person deliberately. As long as these things are done with a good sense of humor, it is OK too.

But what happens when it is done without any respect whatsoever towards the other? For example, in the shocking incidents of ragging in college hostels we often hear about.

Even though I am your teacher, we still can have fun together. But, the moment you (or for that matter, I myself) forget the value of respect and are bent upon doing it only to have fun, I will, regardless of the teacher's dignity, make you change. And, I shall remind you, *gently and strongly, without any feelings of guilt and without any intention to cause any hurt to you*, to treat me with that due respect. And, thus, our relationship in the future shall become healthier and mutually caring. This can be learned and can be done quite assertively too.

8. I have the right to explain my position in a manner I think and feel is most appropriate

An employee in an office is asked to perform a specific task. When the task has been done, the boss does not like the result. Very often, these bosses shout at the subordinate without even giving a chance to the other person to explain the facts.

Say my father asks me to go to the market to get an errand done. Somehow, the task could not be completed the way he wanted it. When I return, without even waiting for my explanation, he starts shouting at me and labels me as irresponsible.

Why do these people not listen to me before choosing to give me a piece of their minds? Just because they are in a position to do so, can they deny the right of the other person to explain his position first? Why do people make assumptions without even considering the facts?

There is a saying in my native language, *"If the person who is serving the meal does not know the limits, should not the person who is eating, know it?"*

Whenever anyone gives me a piece of his mind before allowing me a chance to explain my position, I quietly listen till the other person stops. Then, *I explain my position in a manner I feel most appropriate.* Often, the others have to say sorry to me. See the way assumptions by others are set right when you choose to be assertive.

You and I have the right to explain our position in a manner which we consider as appropriate.

9. I have the right to say 'NO' without feeling guilty

On so many occasions, all of us are placed in situations where we have to say 'No'. But saying so can tend to make us feel guilty too.

My Assertive Human Rights

Someone who is very close to me asks me for a favour. I know his request is based on his genuine needs too. But, because of my past experiences with him, I do want to say 'No' too. In such a case, why should I feel guilty?

I have no intentions to hurt him. Here, truthfully, *I would feel guilty* if I did not say 'No'. Why should I feel guilty at all? I say 'No' and feel happy that I asserted myself. Why not? After all, I do accept the responsibility for my actions.

10. I have the right to ask for a clarification when I don't understand

The classroom can be a good example. The teacher explains something and you do not understand. When you tell him so, the teacher makes you feel guilty by saying, "Oh God! Even after such clear explanations, you don't understand? What's the matter with you?" Thus, you are often made to feel guilty if you did say that you did not understand. This means that most students keep quiet and do not venture to ask even genuine questions. Why should this be so? Can I not ask for a clarification if I did not understand?

Let us see how this dialogue could go on:

"Sorry, sir. I did not understand."

"What's the matter with you? Can't you understand such simple things?" (The answer still happens to be that I did not understand.)

"I am sorry, sir. But, I did not understand."

"What will happen to me if everyone starts behaving like this? After all, what I explained was such a simple thing."

I shall continue to keep looking at the teacher and maintain silence.

Now, it will be the turn of the teacher to get frustrated. "What's the matter with you? Why can't you answer me?"

So I say, "Honestly, sir. I did not understand."

If I continue assertively in this way, the teacher shall have to explain in a manner that I will understand. And, in the process, I have ensured that I have not gathered any more guilt too. The teacher too will stop manipulating me to agree what he has tried with him without even understanding to teach.

I am not too sure what happens in other countries. But, certainly in India, most students choose to remain silent without asking even the most relevant questions so that they are spared the embarrassment after the questions are asked.

Is it not the sacred duty of a teacher to help me to understand? I certainly am not going feel guilty *when I ask for a clarification if I did not understand something.*

I shall do so with my parents, with my bosses and with anyone who has a responsibility to make me understand. Why should I say 'Yes' when my answer is 'No?' And, I shall do so *gently, strongly, without any feelings of guilt, and, without any intentions to hurt the other person.* That, truly, is being assertive. In this process, I shall not only learn better but also prevent others from manipulating me to suit their own purposes.

11. I have the right to ask for what I want, knowing that the other person has the right to refuse

I do have the right to ask for a raise from my boss, as was done in the case of Kumar, the stenographer. The boss too has a right to refuse if he did have a genuine, valid reason to do so. Why should either of them feel guilty while performing their duties? However, in such a transaction, the ones who have no feelings of guilt, shall win in the end.

It is also true that I cannot ask for a raise, unless I am fully convinced that I deserve it. Therefore, where is the question of guilt? Why should there be any fights and ill feelings?

Further, the Biblical saying goes, *"Knock and it shall open."* We may also add, *"Ask and it shall be given to you."*

In the end, remember... *for every right there is a responsiblity too.*

19

Self-awareness Check: Response Style Assessment

> "No one can do inspired work without genuine interest in his subject and understanding of its characteristics."
> ANDREAS FEININGER
> American photographer

The following assessment is designed to help you to evaluate *how others respond to you*. It will aid you in determining how you "come across" to other people who are close to you.

Circle one of the numbers next to each statement to indicate the frequency with which it occurs to you. Do not spend too much time deciding on any answer. Use your first reaction.

	Often	Sometimes	Seldom	Never
1. When some junior breaks an established rule, you confront him by finding out his reasons and working out a solution so that it doesn't happen again.	3	2	1	0
2. People at times draw away from you or fail to make eye contact; they seem edgy or nervous in your presence.	3	2	1	0
3. People state their opinions to you openly.	3	2	1	0
4. People move in and dominate you because you won't stand up for your rights.	3	2	1	0
5. People tend to dismiss your ideas or fail to seek your opinions.	3	2	1	0
6. People at times seem to have a desire to show off a bit more with you than when dealing with others.	3	2	1	0
7. When dealing with you, people become careful, tentative, and guarded.	3	2	1	0
8. People try to avoid you because they don't want to feel guilty or uncomfortable as a result of your apologetic or self-pitying behaviour.	3	2	1	0
9. When you say you will help people to get what they want, they believe you.	3	2	1	0
10. People respect your opinion.	3	2	1	0
11. People rarely disagree with you and avoid crossing you.	3	2	1	0
12. People rarely ask you to take on tough tasks in dealing with people because you are too easy-going.	3	2	1	0
13. People put on protective airs or become patronising because they are afraid to confront you directly; they feel that you can't take it.	3	2	1	0
14. People feel free to come to you when they have a problem to sort out.	3	2	1	0
15. People do not bring their problems or questions to you.	3	2	1	0
16. People try to put you down or embarrass you with humour or subtle contempt.	3	2	1	0
17. Your group is one which people from other groups want to come and join.	3	2	1	0
18. People feel they can break the rules and get away with it and you won't say anything.	3	2	1	0

Self-awareness Check: Response Style Assessment

Among the three columns provided below, enter your score against each serial number.

S. No.	Score	S. No.	Score	S. No.	Score
1		4		2	
3		5		6	
9		8		7	
10		12		11	
14		13		15	
17		18		16	
Total		Total		Total	

The left-hand column indicates your *assertive score*.
The middle column indicates your *passive score*.
The right-hand column indicates your *aggressive score*.
Ideally, the scores should read *18, 0, 0*.

Although these response behaviours by others may be the result of their own needs, your score can help you to be more aware of others' reactions to you. Observing how others treat you, can help you determine what you can do to be more effective in your dealings with them.

If your *assertive* score was high, there is a good chance that people will come to you with their problems, feel comfortable even when they disagree, listen to your ideas, and generally want to work in your group in a cooperative way.

If your *passive* score was high, it may mean that you are using *Theory Y* to your advantage. Being people-oriented is a fine quality, but not when it is misused or abused, resulting in loss of respect from those who work with you.

If your *aggressive* score was high, you probably need to examine the manner in which you establish rules and deal with people. It may mean that you are using *Theory X*. You may want to reflect on how your behaviour is influencing your effectiveness.

Note: You will find explanations of *Theory Y* and *Theory X* in the following pages.

20

Assumptions about People

> *"An optimist is a person who sees a green light everywhere, while the pessimist sees only the red stop light . . . but the truly wise person is colour blind."*
> ALBERT SCHWEITZER
> German missionary

Traditional Theory X	*Theory Y as explained by Douglas McGregor in his book* Human-side of Enterprise.
1. The average person has an inherent dislike for work and will avoid it if he can.	1. Expenditure of physical and mental effort in work is as natural as play or rest, depending on controllable conditions; work may be either a source of satisfaction or dissatisfaction.
2. Because of this dislike for work, most people must be coerced, controlled, directed, threatened, punished to get them to put	2. External control and the threat of punishment are not the only means

Assumptions about People

forth adequate efforts towards the achievement of organisational goals–even the promise of reward is not enough. People will accept and demand more. Only threats will do the trick.
3. The average person prefers to be directed, wishes to avoid responsibility, has little ambition, wants security above all—mediocrity is the sign of the masses.

for bringing about efforts towards objectives.
3. Commitment is a function of rewards associated with their achievement.
4. Under proper conditions, people will not only accept but seek responsibility—avoidance of responsibility, lack of ambition, emphasis on security, are the consequence of experience and not human characteristics.
5. Capacity to exercise imagination, ingenuity, creativity is widely and not narrowly distributed.
6. Intellectual potentials of the average person are being only partially utilised.

Once you understand these concepts, you'll know that the final answer does not lie in remaining either in *Theory X or Theory Y*. These must be considered as two extreme points; a range of attitudes within which to operate. However, in dealing with human elements, it will be always advantageous for a person to begin in Theory Y and when needed, move towards Theory X, till a point of balance is reached.

21

Assertive Personality
(Two Examples)

> "Science is not to be regarded merely as a storehouse of facts to be used for material purposes, but as one of the human endeavours to be ranked with the arts and religion as the guide and expression of man's fearless quest for truth."
>
> SIR RICHARD GREGORY
> British scientist

Let us consider two examples. First, a *nation*, and then a *person*.

The Second World War came to an end after the Allied forces dropped two atom bombs during August 1945, one in Hiroshima and the other in Nagasaki. Japan, on all apparent accounts was finished. They were completely devastated, dominated and controlled by the Western nations. They were not allowed to raise an armed force too. In the years that ensued, what really happened to them? Were they finished? Are they?

Assertive Personality

After the Second World War, the Japanese had to redefine the war itself. The cause that made them engage themselves in a war, the cause itself, had not been eliminated. They had suffered humiliation and defeat. Is it possible for any nation to forget them easily?

Why does anyone, be it a nation or a person, engage in war? *To win over the other.*

What does 'winning over the other' really mean? *Gaining mastery and superiority over the other.*

Are all the killings and the pain caused to millions, essential in a war? Are they? History records that wars have always been fought through killings and destruction. Pain, suffering, deprivations have always been associated with them.

Because of the specific conditions within which they were bound, the Japanese had to redefine the war. When they did it, they found: *"A war is fought to gain superiority over another. At a national level, the only superiority that is worth it, is in the economic arena."*

They must have asked themselves, "Is it essential to kill others to gain economic superiority over them? Are we really interested in it?" The answer was a clear *No*.

Therefore, the question now became how they could gain economic superiority over other nations. When they thought deeply about it, the answer must have become not only clear to them, but also very apparent. *"Gain mastery and superiority over them in the economic arena. Fight them in the business spheres."* This was the starting point of scoring over their opponents.

How to gain mastery over others, and that too without having to kill anyone in the process? The answer now became clear: *"Capture the economy."*

From then on, all their efforts were directed towards economic victory. And, how marvellously they did it! Now, they were lucky because they did not have to spend their resources in maintaining armed forces.

In the Western world, most of the sports events are directed towards defeating the opponent, even to the extent of harming the other. We could consider *boxing* as an example. Two people keep hitting and injuring each other. In the end, whoever succeeds in landing more blows on the other, is declared the winner. And, they are happy to call it a sport.

The Western world has even forgotten the motto of the Olympic Games which says, "*Just as in life, the most important thing is not to win, but to participate well.*"

Now, consider the case of Japan. To them, a sport equivalent to Western boxing is judo. There are many other popular, Japanese martial arts like kung fu and karate too.

Unlike in boxing, a person engaged in judo is only interested in self-defence. He has no interest whatsoever in hurting the other. And, in essence, for achieving this goal, that individual who learns judo need not even be physically stronger than the opponent. Even frail-looking young girls and old monks could become experts in judo. The real strength, according to them, does not relate to the physical components. Instead, it comes from directing the mental and spiritual energies. For this reason, those learning judo or other Eastern martial arts, undergo long years of training in mental disciplines before they are even taught the basics of the actions.

Check the ways in which the Japanese have fought the world economy and gained remarkable victories after their defeat in 1945.

Once upon a time, automobiles to the world meant those from the USA. Today, there is the considerable presence of Japanese automobiles even in the USA. In other countries, Japanese have virtually conquered this market. The have even set up automobile plants all over the Western countries. If you have ever visited Africa, or read about the conditions there, you'll know that the Japanese have held complete sway in the automobile market there, for so many years. As of now, they are still very much in the leading position, although there are other players like Korea too, who are neighbours to the Japanese.

In the field of electronics, the less said the better. We could possibly write a long thesis on this. But, it would be sufficient if you observe how *assertive* the Japanese are.

Apparently, the Japanese are *very gentle*, but they are *strong too*. They do not demonstrate any *intentions to hurt the other* and *they have no reasons to feel guilty too*. Do not all these qualities fit well within our definition of assertiveness? Would you say they are 'passive' or 'aggressive?'

Japanese methods of business negotiations are very well-known now to the rest of the world. They specialise in tiring out the opponent and win in the end. The Western world too, being

Assertive Personality

progressive, have adopted many lessons learned from the Japanese for their own benefit.

There was a time when all management education meant the skills that came from the Americans. Today, even the Americans are learning lessons from the Japanese.

After gaining independence in 1947, India, except in rare cases, had kept their economy closed from the foreign powers for many years. For decades, the nation had only three models of cars. And the users had to remain content with whatever quality was rationed out to them. In the case of a specific car model, the waiting period between booking the car and getting the delivery, used to be more than 10 years.

Today, what is the position? All automobile dealers are advertising ready delivery with attractive, easy, instalment payments. Who was responsible for this change?

The *Japanese*. The moment, Suzuki introduced their 'Maruti' models, the Indian equations changed. Today, they are the market leaders. And, other automobile manufacturers have been forced to improve their models. Those who could not do so, had to bow out and close down their plants.

Another major area of Japanese presence is in the electronics field. Look at the manifestations of being *assertive*.

Now, let us consider an example of the assertive person; an individual.

For over two centuries, the British ruled India with an iron hand. The Indians were their slaves. It used to be said that the sun never set in the British empire. What is the position today? And, where and how did it begin?

Mahatma Gandhi used to be called a 'half-naked fakir'. He led the Indian people to fight, using *non-violence*. Initially, hardly anyone could understand him. But, he proved his point first in South Africa and later became the Father of the Indian nation.

Gandhi held no ill-will for the British. His only demand was complete Independence for India. Every punishment meted out to him and his people, were met by non-violence.

They locked Gandhi in jails for many years. He suffered quietly. He would never utter any violent words against the British. When it became necessary for him to assert his point, he took to complete fasting. He refused to eat for days until his demand was granted by the authorities.

The British, masters of many wars, were at a complete loss to fight this *half-naked fakir*.

Finally, the opponents had to give up. In the process, there was no loss of goodwill between the Indians and the British too.

Mahatma, Mohandas Karamchand Gandhi, was a perfect example of an ASSERTIVE personality.

After Gandhi, there were many examples of such assertive leaders too. Martin Luther King Jr. and Nelson Mandela are two who are well-known and worthy of mention.

22

Developing an Assertive Personality

> "They always say that time changes things, but you actually have to change them yourself."
>
> ANDY WARHOL
> American artist

Developing an assertive personality calls for paying attention to eight major components. These are progressive and hierarchical in order.

We have to begin with item 1 and master it first. Then proceed on to item 2 and further on.

1. Building self-esteem.
2. Knowing how to listen.
3. Taking risks.
4. Knowing how to say NO.
5. Knowing how to give a constructive feedback.
6. Handling criticism.

7. Knowing how to express and receive a positive feedback.
8. Knowing what you want.

Let us understand each of them in a little more detail.

BUILDING SELF-ESTEEM

Most of us are brought up to believe that modesty is a great virtue, and that pride and boasting should be avoided at all costs. The usual result is that many people find it difficult to accept compliments about what they do and to take credit for their accomplishments.

To succeed in life, it is important that you see yourself in a positive manner. A way to do this is to allow yourself to feel satisfied when you function at your best, and acknowledge your strengths and abilities. You and I have to feel good, when we know we have done something well. Often, others may not even notice our good work. Even if they do, they may not even bother to acknowledge it you.

It is also harder to see the best in others when we focus on the negative aspects within ourselves.

Promotion, recognition, and power often go to those people who are self-confident. Modesty, for example, can work against you when you are selling something to others.

Warning: An inflated self-image or a boastfully aggressive self-portrayal can be as damaging as excessive modesty.

Essentially, it is important that you should develop genuine self-respect deep within you as the first step towards developing assertiveness.

KNOWING HOW TO LISTEN

Most people do not possess effective listening skills. There is much more to listening than what is generally being perceived.

LISTENING is the process of using our *Eyes, Ears,* and the *Senses,* to *UNDERSTAND* the *Meanings* (both literal and hidden) and the *Feelings* of the speaker.

Today, top corporations the world over are beginning to recognise the roles of good listeners in saving company time, money and increasing productivity.

Results in any organised activity, be it living together in a small family or working for a large corporation, depend on *UNDERSTANDING, COOPERATION* and *TRUST.* If so, *Listening,*

Developing an Assertive Personality

Observation and the *ability to ask the Right Questions* become extremely important skills.

Make a closer observation of the meanings conveyed in the following quote attributed to William Stringfellow which appeared in the Readers' Digest:

> *Listening is a rare happening among human beings. You cannot listen to the word another is speaking if you are preoccupied with your appearance, or with impressing the other, or are trying to decide what you are going to say when the other person stops talking, or are debating about whether what is being said is true or relevant or agreeable.*
>
> *Listening is a primitive act of love in which a person gives himself to another's word, making himself accessible and vulnerable to that word.*

When you improve your listening skills, it shall lead to:

— Improved working relationships with people.
— Getting projects completed efficiently.
— Results obtained more efficiently and faster.
— Mistakes reduced or even eliminated.
— Quality ensured.
— Productivity enhanced.
— Profits assured.

An *assertive person* will *listen* to the *needs, ideas,* and *feelings* of those persons that he/she comes across.

When someone is talking, it is easy to spend the time thinking about how you will respond rather than listening to what is being said. In this process, information gets distorted and misinterpreted and this results in misunderstanding and frustration. The temptation, very often, is to jump to conclusions and tell the other person what to do, rather than hearing him out to understand the situation.

Failure to listen leads to many kinds of problems:

— People acting on what they thought was said rather than understanding what was really said.
— Agreeing to ideas that weren't truly understood.
— Completing tasks incorrectly because one doesn't want to appear stupid by admitting that he or she did not listen.
— Misinterpreting an assignment, therefore doing it incorrectly.

You may not agree with the other person's point of view. But that should not prevent you from paying respectful attention and asking thoughtful questions. You will learn more. More important, it is a sound basis for human relations too.

Good listening includes indicating your *understanding* to the other person.

And . . . understanding does not mean agreement.

Develop the habits of listening well, indicating your understanding to the speaker, and then, speaking what you want to. Now, the other person cannot say that you haven't understood him/her. Thus arguments are averted, and you shall have created a condition for being *more assertive*.

TAKING RISKS

Taking risks include :

Speaking up for what you believe,
Asking for what you want,
Stating your conditions and limits, and,
Expressing your expectations of others.

These are considered risk-taking because people have a mistaken belief that others will respond to them adversely and will judge the speaker in a negative way. People are also led to believe that asking for what one wants is not acceptable behaviour, and their doing so is dangerous.

Some people have this belief; "Any good person will know what's required of him/her without my having to explain in detail to him/her." And "if he/she had brains, he/she would know that I don't like the habit of people coming even five minutes late." Because of these assumptions, we tend to believe that others should understand what they are expected to do without "my having to explain it to them every time." We tend to expect that others should be able to read our minds. It is a sure way to set ourselves up for frustration.

Assertive persons will take initiatives, let others know *what* they want done, *how* they want it done, and *why* it is important. Passively hoping that others will guess what is wanted could lead to resentment and poor time management.

Another area that seems to cause problems by our not letting the other persons know specifically what we want, is when we delegate tasks. To perform a task well, it is important that we say *what* has to be done, *when* it is to be done, and *why* it is important. Failure to take time to clarify the details often causes failure in the following-through.

At another extreme are our specific demands that others should perform the tasks exactly the same way "I want it done." Such arbitrary and dictatorial ways may provoke surface compliance. But it creates an inner resistance and resentment which remains hidden, looking out for opportunities to express itself.

Part of risk-taking is *setting limits*. We sometimes come across situations where we have to interact with people who are *hostile, pushy* or *demanding*. When dealing with such people, we have the responsibility to let others know how their behaviour is affecting us and suggest another way to handle the situation.

When we set our boundaries, let others know where we stand and how we want to be treated, the process of being truly assertive would have begun. It also opens out a path to gain respect. *When you do not set your limits, you allow others to pick on you. Is it not difficult not to walk over someone who lies down in front of you!*

On the other extreme, there are people who are extremely sensitive. They take offence easily, and become defensive. *"What cannot be cured, has to be endured,"* goes the popular saying. Therefore, *without any intentions to cause any hurt to the other person, and without any feelings of guilt, I shall continue to be gentle and strong in my behaviour."* Isn't it what assertiveness is all about?

KNOWING HOW TO SAY NO

As an individual who seeks success in life, you need to rely heavily on your ability to meet goals, implement plans, distribute resources, mediate and negotiate within your sphere of responsibility. To do these, you also need to establish boundaries, state what is acceptable to you and express what is *not* acceptable to you. It is also important for you to know what you are *willing to* and are *able to* do with your limited resource of time.

The ability to say *No* is crucial in three areas:

i) *Saying No to unwanted tasks imposed by colleagues and superiors.* Without this ability, you may be flooded with tasks that are not your responsibility and thus, you may deprive yourself of the time to perform those tasks that you are responsible for, more effectively.

ii) *Saying No to being imposed with unrealistic deadlines*
Being able to prevent yourself from imposed with unrealistic deadlines could mean that you are able to complete your tasks on time, and prevent yourself from being blamed as ineffective by others.

This reminds me of an incident that I must share with you. Many years ago, I was working as a supervisor in a factory. I had a boss who was foreigner (British). He was considered a terror by other supervisors. I was warned by my colleagues about his ways even before I had interacted with that boss.

One morning, the boss called me to his cabin and threw a bunch of papers in front of me and said, "Now take these. Study them, prepare a report, have it completed and ready on my table by 4.00 p.m. tomorrow. Chop. Chop. Now go."

What am I supposed to do now? Run away without even knowing what deadline I was agreeing to? Do I not have a natural right to examine the task before agreeing to a deadline for its completion? Other supervisors had succumbed to the habit of passively agreeing to tasks without even a basic examination of the work. Because of this, when they were unable to complete those tasks satisfactorily within the time, they were also being blamed as ineffective. Am I to get into such a rut right at the start of my career?

I stood in front of my boss, quietly reading the papers to assess the responsibility given to me and the possible time that may be required to complete it. My boss was curiously watching me. But he did not say anything.

After I examined the papers, I knew that it would take me three days to complete that report and I would have to work after office hours for it too.

Therefore, I spoke to him *assertively:* "Sir, I shall have it completed by 4:00 p.m. tomorrow, if you insist."

He must have known I had something more to say. So he asked, "Then, what is the problem?"

"But I personally feel that it will take me three days to prepare a complete report." Possibly, this could have been the first time a supervisor was speaking to him in this fashion.

Developing an Assertive Personality

He stared at me coolly and asked, "If I do give you three days to prepare this report, will you promise to give me a complete report?"

"Yes, Sir."

Most people may not have the courage to say this kind of "*Yes.*" Therefore, they end up saying, "I will try, Sir." This kind of *trying* doesn't work in reality.

When a person says, "I will try" there is an inner doubt present in that reply. The word *try* is used for connecting it up later with a *"but I failed."* If you don't want to believe me, check for yourself.

My answer was, *"Yes, Sir. I shall have it completed and ready by 9:00 a.m. on Thursday."*

"Very well then. You may go now."

For the next three nights I hardly slept. I even had to take active help from a friend who was a senior manager in an office. In those three days, I learned many things about how to prepare a proper report. I became excited about my work too.

Now, I was anxious and ready to meet my boss at 9:00 a.m. on Thursday. A few minutes before the deadline ended, I knocked, walked in and said: "Sir, here is the report I promised you," and laid it on his table. He simply said, "You may go now." And I quietly walked out.

In another hour or so, he called me to his cabin. As I walked in, I could see a smile on his face.

He offered me a seat and said very pleasantly: "Very good. You have written a good report. Now tell me, how did you learn how to write such good reports?"

Feeling relieved and happy, I replied: "Sir, I really did not know how to write such a report till you asked me. To make sure it would be acceptable, I hardly slept during the last three nights. I even took the help of a friend who is a manager. I am glad you liked it."

I need not go into details on how the rapport between the two of us grew in the months ahead. But I must tell you about his behaviour with me after this incident. He would walk into my cabin and ask me, "How long do you think it will take you to complete a report on this?" From then on, I could ask for whatever time I wanted. He knew that the job would get completed. And, I had acquired a rapport with him. In the process, I grew professionally faster than all my colleagues.

Therefore, being assertive is to be able to *say No to being imposed with unrealistic deadlines.*

iii) *Saying No to manipulative attempts by others to suit their own purposes*

People are always trying to manipulate others to suit their own purposes. Maybe it is natural too. But, what happens to me if I do not know how to say *No* in such situations? Without this ability you and I shall be subjected to experiences of many things in life that we shall regret later.

SAYING NO

Here are some guidelines:

—*Say No, firmly and calmly, without unnecessarily adding "I am sorry" if it is not called for.*

You don't have to always say sorry for anything and everything. If you do, you are expressing a sad feeling about your reply and are unhappy about it. Listen! If you are truly feeling sad and unhappy about your actions, then do not engage in it.

To this explanation of mine, you may tell me, "Oh! I do not mean that I am really sorry. I am just saying so." Don't ever express a feeling like this unless there is some truth behind it. Otherwise, the chances are that you will turn out to be a perfect hypocrite; someone who acts pleasant with dishonest intentions. This is the reason behind those cases of *Mona*, and *the friend* who refused the loan of money. There was no 'sorry'.

There is nothing wrong in saying *sorry*. On the contrary, it is often extremely courteous to say so. But you never need to say it unless you feel it or have valid reasons for feeling so. Remember, this explanation is offered within the context of learning to be assertive.

—*Say No, followed by a straightforward explanation without any feelings of guilt.*

"I cannot undertake this additional work now, because the assignment I am working on currently has a deadline for completion by tomorrow evening at 5:00 p.m. I will need every moment I can snatch for completing it.

—*Say No, and then (if possible) give a choice or alternative*

Personally, I won't be able to undertake this additional assignment. But if you could give me the support of an operator

Developing an Assertive Personality

for a full day, I could guide him to get it completed within your deadline.

—*Make an empathetic listening statement, and then say No.*

What you have told me is that I must help you to have your loan squared up by Thursday afternoon. Otherwise, you could land in serious difficulties. I understand your position and I fully sympathise with you. But, I will not be able to help you in this matter.

—*Say Yes. Then give your reasons for not doing it or your alternative solution.*

Of course I shall help you. Certainly. But it can only be that I shall introduce you to him. Beyond this, I can't do anything more. You will have to persuade him to accept your proposal. It may also be possible, if you could persuade the Regional Office to send me a sanction on your behalf. For this, you will need to meet Mr. Fernando and have it sanctioned by him. I won't be able to do this on your behalf.

The above approach is known as *'Yes But'* or *'Yes If'* or *'Conditional'* approach.

—Then you could always use the 'PERSISTENT RESPONSE' method when you know that you are being manipulated by others. This is also known as the 'BROKEN RECORD' technique. (The needle in the gramophone keeps playing on the same groove of the record, again and again.)

"I understand how feel. But I won't able to help you in this matter."

"I know what you are asking me. But, I am not interested."

"I do not want to undertake this assignment."

"You could be right. But, I cannot accept your suggestion."

KNOWING HOW TO GIVE CONSTRUCTIVE FEEDBACK

Most people have difficulty in providing corrective feedbacks because they find it difficult to accept it themselves.

People often respond to *how the criticism is stated* rather than understanding what is being stated.

Generally, people do want improve at what they are doing. But, when the criticism is stated with a *fault-finding attitude, and expressed with judgments and threats,* it is understandable that the person receiving it may respond with *anger, hurt, or defensiveness.*

Constructive Feedback:
Is stated in specific terms instead of vague, general ones.
Is directed at behaviour rather than on personalities.
Is an observation of events rather than labelling of emotional judgements.
Shall focus on a coaching style instead of putting-down others.
Shall allow the receiver to solve his or her problems.

Giving and Receiving Feedback

1. *Focus feedback on BEHAVIOUR rather than on the PERSONALITY.* It is important that we refer to what a person does rather than comment on what we imagine he or she is. Thus, we might say to a person *"You talked considerably in this meeting,"* rather than saying, *"You are a chatterbox."* It is less threatening to a person to hear comments about his behaviour rather than his personality.

2. *Focus feedback on OBSERVATIONS rather than on INFERENCES.* Observations refer to what we can see or hear in the behaviour of another person, while, inferences refer to the interpretations and conclusions which we make from what we see or hear.

3. *Focus feedback on DESCRIPTION rather than on JUDGEMENT.* The effort to describe represents a process for reporting what occurred, while judgement refers to an evaluation in terms of good or bad, right or wrong, nice or not nice.

4. *Focus feedback on BEHAVIOUR related to a SPECIFIC SITUATION preferably to the "HERE and NOW", rather than to a behaviour in the abstract, placing it in the "THERE and THEN".* By sharing ideas and information, we shall leave the other person free to decide for himself in the light of his/her own goals in a specific situation at a specific time.

5. *Focus feedback on EXPLORATION of ALTERNATIVES rather than ANSWERS or SOLUTIONS.* The more we can focus on a variety of procedures and means for attaining a particular goal the less likely we shall be to accept a specific alternative solution prematurely.

6. *Focus feedback on the VALUE it may have on the RECIPIENT and not on the 'release' it may provide the person giving the feedback.* To overload a person with a feedback is to reduce the possibility of effectiveness of what he may use out of what he receives.

7. Focus feedback at the RIGHT TIME and PLACE so that personal data can be shared effectively.
   Because the reception and use of personal feedback involves many possible emotional reactions, it is important that we become sensitive about when it is appropriate to provide the feedback.
8. Now we come to listening to and receiving Feedbacks. We must learn to listen to the feedback in terms of WHAT is being said rather than WHY it is being said.
   To make assumptions about the motives of the person giving the feedback may prevent us from listening or may cause us to distort what is being said. In short, if I question "why" a person gives me a feedback, I may not listen and understand "what" he says.

In short, the giving and receiving of feedbacks require courage, skill, understanding and respect for the self and for others.

HANDLING CRITICISM

People *do* criticise. They *do* find ways to find fault with whatever I do. It is impossible to eliminate it altogether.

Therefore, developing an assertive personality would call for developing the ability to face and handle criticism from others without becoming defensive or upset. There are several factors that lead you and I to handle criticism emotionally rather than effectively.

- Taking criticism *personally* instead of seeing it as a possible corrective feedback.
- Failing to separate the *relevant* from irrelevant criticism.
- Reading into criticism some *message* that isn't there.
- Seeing the criticism as an invitation to get *angry* or to judge oneself *harshly* or *reprimandingly*.
- Failing to understand *specifics* and *examples* of what is being criticised.
- Believing that expressing criticism is *bad* or *wrong*.

It is only natural that we often react to criticism emotionally rather than objectively. To be assertive, it is important that we learn to accept criticism and find ways of benefiting from them.

Do not answer back immediately. Wait, think about it and then, if needed, come up objective reactions.

If there are *any corrective feedbacks present* in the criticism, *accept* them. Reject the rest by remembering, *"God forgive them. They do not know what they are saying."* If there is any suitable opportunity to clarify your position, only then offer an appropriate explanation.

Look for the *relevant facts* and reject the rest.

Do not read *too much meaning* into most of the criticism. However, you must look for those that are meaningful.

There is no need to get unnecessarily angry or to punish yourself unduly. After all, *to err is human and to forgive is divine.*

Seek out the specific facts and benefit from them.

If someone offers you a criticism, you don't have to always consider it as *bad or wrong.*

Learning to recognise the type of criticism that is being directed towards you and handling them more effectively, calls for becoming aware of your feelings when it happens to you.

Some people criticise to feel 'one-up', to justify their own position by annoying you.

Others do so when they are themselves feeling frustrated, and therefore use you as a way to release their negative feelings.

Still others do so to gain information about problems that need to be solved.

All these and more could be handled effectively, if you are willing to think deeply and avoid becoming emotional about them.

KNOWING HOW TO EXPRESS AND RECEIVE A POSITIVE FEEDBACK

Some persons experience difficulties in giving positive feedbacks to others because of the beliefs they hold, such as:

"Why should I show my appreciation? They too get paid for the work they do just like me, don't they?"

"When you give too much attention to others, they climb on your head and sit there."

"It is not my job to make others feel good. It's my job to get the work done."

However, an assertive person shall always remember the value of appreciation.

Positive Feedback, which is commonly known as *appreciation*, in its best application, is *reinforcing the self-worth another person feels*. People are motivated when they are appreciated, treated with respect, and given due credit for a job well done. It is the same for you and for me too.

When you realise how good you feel when you are acknowledged and recognised for having accomplished something worthwhile, you qualify yourself for giving a similar satisfaction to others. Such a realisation and practice will lead to positive responses from people around.

KNOWING WHAT YOU WANT OUT OF LIVING

The final building block for managing yourself assertively lies in knowing *what you want, setting goals, and developing plans to accomplish them*. Often it is tempting to sit back and wish that things were different. But people who waste their time on "if only . . . " are not doing what they need to do to become successful.

A truly assertive personality shall rely heavily on persistence, perseverance, and be unwilling to give up despite obstacles.

The approach each of us shall apply, will depend on our specific values, goals and needs. These also call for flexibility and versatility in our styles and behaviour.

Finally, setting up long-range goals for all the seven areas of your development—*Family, People, Career, Money, Body, Mind* and *Self-actualisation*—will go a long way in obtaining the position you cherish from your life.

Your need for success, shall require you to plan effective strategies for developing an assertive personality. (Later, we shall engage ourselves in specific workshops for each of these seven areas.)

23

Acquiring an Assertive Personality: Where are You Now?

> "It's true that tomorrow may be better—or worse. But today may not be so bad. You must appreciate the miracle you're alive right now and forget about how, or if, you are going to live tomorrow."
>
> ROD STEIGER
> American film star

Circle the number that most nearly describes how you see yourself in relation to each type of behaviour.

Acquiring an Assertive Personality: Where are You Now?

	All the time				Never	
1. When I am disturbed about what someone is doing, I can say so.	5	4	3	2	1	0
2. When someone starts talking right in the middle of my conversation, I am able to express my feelings about the interruption.	5	4	3	2	1	0
3. When someone goes on talking over the phone without considering my position, I am able to cut him/her short assertively when I am busy.	5	4	3	2	1	0
4. When a person purposely annoys me continually, I am able to express my displeasure.	5	4	3	2	1	0
5. When someone I respect expresses opinions with which I strongly disagree, I state my point of view.	5	4	3	2	1	0
6. I am inclined to be too apologetic.	0	1	2	3	4	5
7. When a colleague criticises me unjustly, I am able to express my point of view.	5	4	3	2	1	0
8. When necessary, I am able to contradict a domineering person.	5	4	3	2	1	0
9. If I hear that someone is spreading false rumours about me, I can go directly to him or her to correct the situation.	5	4	3	2	1	0
10. I am able to give compliments and recognition to those within my group.	5	4	3	2	1	0
11. I am able to ask people to do unpleasant tasks.	5	4	3	2	1	0
12. I am able to give a corrective feedback to those within my group.	5	4	3	2	1	0
13. I am able to handle an angry person in a calm and gentle way.	5	4	3	2	1	0
14. I am able to handle criticism effectively.	5	4	3	2	1	0
15. I state my conditions and expectations to those who work with me.	5	4	3	2	1	0

16. I generally express my feelings.	5	4	3	2	1	0
17. I avoid unpleasant situations for fear that I won't be able to handle them effectively.	0	1	2	3	4	5
18. I remain calm and rational in stressful situations.	5	4	3	2	1	0
19. I am able to state unpleasant things about a colleague (when truthfully needed) without much weeping about it.	5	4	3	2	1	0
20. If I am asked to judge a dispute within two persons in my group, I feel that I can do a comfortable, yet reasonably good job about it.	5	4	3	2	1	0

Now, review your assessment from this exercise:

The behaviour that I am happy with and want to continue doing.
S.No(s) _____

How do these types of behaviour affect me?
_____
_____
_____

The behaviour that I will need to improve:
_____
_____

Action statements for me to make these changes:
_____
_____
_____

Specific ways by which I am going to make these changes:
_____
_____
_____

24

Motivation

> "If our life lacks a constant magic it is because we choose to observe our acts and lose ourselves in consideration of their imagined form, instead of being impelled by their force."
> ANTONIN ARTAUD
> French playwright

In our definition of *success*, we observed that the key word was *goals*. And, by implication, it is also the key to *motivation*.

When we seek out definitions of *Motivation*, we shall find several components that are commonly stated. Three of the essential ones among them are:

1. *Motivation involves desires or needs.*
2. *Motivation involves expectations and beliefs.*
3. *Motivation involves action.*

Every successful leader throughout the history of government, education, military, religion and business, benefited from their understanding of *motivation* to lead people towards action. Simply stated, the process involved discovering a basic human need—a drive, a desire, or an emotion that was strong enough to trigger people to action. Once that need was discovered, then the leader selected a triggering device to activate it, to turn it into a powerful force. Now all he had to do was to convince others to believe and create expectations that the need shall be fulfilled.

GROWTH NEEDS* (Being Values, these are METANEEDS)	SELF-ACTUALISATION Truth Goodness Beauty Liveliness Individuality Perfection Necessity Completion Justice Order Simplicity Richness Playfulness Effortlessness Self-sufficiency Meaningfulness
	SELF-ESTEEM
	ESTEEM BY OTHERS
	LOVE & BELONGING
BASIC NEEDS Deficiency Needs	SAFETY & SECURITY
	PHYSIOLOGICAL Air, Water, Food, Shelter, Sleep, Sex.

THE EXTERNAL ENVIRONMENT
Preconditions for Need Satisfaction
Freedom, Justice, Orderliness,
Challenge (Stimulation)

Growth Needs are all equally important.
They are not hierarchical in nature.

We could consider the numerous revolutions around the world as perfect examples of motivation on a grand scale. On a much smaller scale, we could observe how a mother succeeds in making the child perform well. The popular cartoon series of 'Popeye the Sailor' and his 'can of spinach' is a fine example, intended to make little children eat that bland stuff.

Needs and their satisfaction are common denominations in any relationships. *Needs, Desires, Expectations,* and *Beliefs* lead people to *Actions*.

In 1952, Dr. Abraham Maslow wrote *Motivation and Personality*. The explanations offered by him were profound and are still accepted as the basics for any study of motivation.

Dr. Maslow gave us a hierarchy of needs that influence human behaviour. While trying to understand this theory, we must remember that they are stated hierarchically and are classified in successively subordinate grades.

PHYSIOLOGICAL NEEDS

The most basic needs of a person is to breathe oxygen, and to have water and food. This grouping also includes biological requirements for warmth, shelter, elimination of the body wastes and sexual fulfilment.

A person who is frantically looking out for fulfilling these needs will be prepared to accept any kind of employment. Man will kill to get water; he will even resort to cannibalism to avoid starving. Anyone who has the experience of saving a drowning man will tell you how crazy the man could become while scrambling for air to breathe.

SAFETY AND SECURITY NEEDS

A person may continue to remain engaged in performing dangerous duties as long as his physiological needs are not fulfilled. But, once he gains a confirmed job, when the employer cannot kick him out any day, he has reasonable assurance that these needs shall continue to be regularly fulfilled. Thus, at this point, the Safety and Security Needs shall become relevant to him.

We frequently encounter man's safety needs in more subtle and disguised forms. They include insistence on fair play, desire for job satisfaction, job protection, a feeling of being free from injury—both physical and emotional. These could be noticed in every case of people living together in one form or another.

Ultimately everyone seeks their own sense of security.

The first two levels of needs are basic. Others gain importance only after there is reasonable assurance of these being satisfied.

LOVE AND BELONGING

Now, the needs for social acceptance, for belonging, for togetherness, for friendship and for love, become more prominent. These are also the needs that prompt more people to want a bigger home, a bigger car, more fashionable clothes, and of course, more money.

Even the reason why the majority of people agree to get married is to fulfil their needs for Love and Belonging. Becoming a member of a trade union in the workplace too is prompted by this.

However, it is also true that a specific need ceases to exert a great influence on the individual, once there is a reasonable assurance of its regular fulfilment. What happens to the behaviour of an employee once his job is confirmed and he is settled in a secure employment?

Motivation is a regularly changing programme within each of us. Say there is a serious conflict within the family and the members are at loggerheads, fighting and even hurting each other. Suddenly, they perceive a serious threat to their safety needs, like a fire in the building. Then their behaviour will change and all of them will work in cooperation to fulfil their more important basic needs of safety.

Such changes in our needs are essential and regular.

SELF-ESTEEM/ESTEEM BY OTHERS

These needs are essentially a need for self-respect.

Our esteem needs compel us to gain social acceptance and public recognition. As and when we know that we have achieved something ourselves, the need gets gratified. Conversely, the opposite can lead to loss of motivation too.

No one truly does anything merely for others. Whatever they do to helping others is always done to fulfil their own needs.

SELF-ACTUALISATION

The highest in the need hierarchy, the need for fulfilment of the self, comes to the forefront only after all other needs are reasonably satisfied. It cannot find optimal expression while a person is hungry, fearful for his safety, or feeling rejected by others. Most people, therefore, experience a limited opportunity for this last set of needs.

This discussion on Motivation could be taken to great depths. It has been done by innumerable wise people all over the world too. For our purpose, we must gain a basic idea on why we behave the way we do. Therefore, a limited discussion will suffice.

In conclusion, we could even say that when a person strives to be good, he is doing so to preserve himself.

25

Approaches to Mobilise the Motive Forces

> *"Nothing worth a damn is ever done as a matter of principle. If it is worth doing, it is done because it is worth doing. If it is not, it's done as a matter of principle."*
> JAMES T. EVANS
> American lawyer

The secret to successful living—to zestful, purposeful existence—is in maintaining a balance between *the emotional* and *the logical powers*—between *the right* and *the left brain*, between *theory Y* and *theory X*—that are our natural inheritance.

Logic, or intellect, deals with theory and with probabilities. Our emotions deal with imagination, with dreams, and extend us beyond what is probable, to expand the scope of what is possible.

One is the accelerator. The other is the governor or the brake.

Without either, we are incomplete; and without both, we are nothing.

In our attempts to motivate someone, or even the self, we tend to use two extreme approaches. Let us first consider these two universal ones.

FEAR MOTIVATION

This is the oldest system or type of motivation known to man. It impels a person to act because he/she is afraid of the consequences if he/she fails to act.

Most of us are introduced to fear motivation at an early age. If we disobeyed our parents, we got a beating. Much of the discipline enforced in the school, at work or in public places, uses this approach. Of course much of this discipline need not necessarily be associated with physical punishments. Withdrawal of privileges such as pocket money, no TV, no new clothes or even non-cooperation, are common ways to apply fear motivation.

Many a husband, or wife or child controls his/her behaviour, even abstains from his/her favourite pastimes, not because he/she had become a puritan at heart and in practice, but because of the consequences at home.

Many a law enforcement authority has stated that the crime rate would fall if every potential lawbreaker knew, with a great certainty, that he would be caught and punished.

In the industry and business, this type of motivation is used in the form of reduced wages, lay-offs, retrenchment and even dismissal.

Fear limits and retards the efforts of people. Under fear, the performances could be, at the most, second-rate.

Fear motivation works on the more basic needs; those for physical comfort, for freedom, for security and for social acceptance. Most of these are easily satisfied. There is hardly any instance where this fear has spurred an individual to higher achievements, personal growth, or development of his potential for success.

INCENTIVE MOTIVATION

The opposite of fear is incentive. It impels a person to act with the promise of rewards for achieving the objectives. The effect of incentive motivation can also be seen in all walks of life.

When a newborn baby cries, it is fed or given other kinds of attention it needs. It doesn't take long for the baby to learn that if it behaves in a certain manner, it will be rewarded.

As a person grows, the methods become more sophisticated. He accepts work for the rewards of life—food, shelter, clothing and the countless things that money can bring.

People even use self-denial as a "reverse" form of incentive motivation. They withhold enjoyments until they achieve ("I will not go out to play until the cleaning is completed"), thus hoping to spur themselves to be motivated.

In social and recreational life, people engage in tasks for the applause and appreciation from his/her group.

Perhaps the most classic example of incentive motivation is the *carrot and the stick;* the donkey pulling the cart because a carrot is dangled on a stick before its nose, and the stick itself tied on its back. There is no doubt that the cart will move forward, provided the stick is short enough, the carrot is tempting enough, the load in the cart is light enough and the donkey is hungry enough.

In cases where a person's behaviour pattern started from *physical, security* or *social needs,* once the 'appetite' is quenched, incentives have a less effect on him/her. Many a time, what starts out as a reward gradually becomes a right and then, there is no end to the increased rewards that will be demanded.

Incentive motivation cannot satisfy the highest needs of an individual: the self-actualisation needs. It does not alter the individual's basic attitudes towards life in general and specifically towards himself.

ATTITUDE MOTIVATION

Any approach to motivation that can create meaning and purpose within a person must appeal to the basic attitudes.

Attitude motivation is based on a true understanding of human behaviour.

You and I can certainly change some of our basic attitudes towards *the self* and towards *others*. It is possible, but it may not be very easy.

We will be required to deal with lingering attitudes, which were formed over long periods of time. Thus, altering them too

Approaches to Mobilise the Motive Forces

will take time. Occasionally, we could even become frustrated in the process. But, it will help us to remember that *attitudes are nothing more than habits of thought*. Because habits are always developed, certainly, they can be changed and new ones developed too.

When a person changes his/her attitudes towards *family, friends and work*, and, most importantly, towards *the self and life in general*, he/she shall alter the basic structures of his/her personality.

26

Planned Personality Development

> "What is divine in Man is elusive and impalpable, and he is easily tempted to embody it in a concrete form—a church, a country, a social system, a leader—so that he may realise it with less effort and serve it with more profit. Yet... the attempt to externalise the kingdom of heaven in a temporal shape must end in disaster. Those who set out for it alone, will reach it together, *and those who seek it in company will perish by themselves."*
>
> HUGH KINGSMILL
> British writer

Life is a journey, not a destination; a flowing, changing process in which nothing is fixed.
 Human development, too, is an ongoing process. It is always partial and incomplete. No person is fully developed or undeveloped. Neither are communities. Neither are nations.

ALL NATIONS AND PERSONS ARE DEVELOPING

Development implies the capacity an individual acquires to solve his/her problems by calling upon his currently available resources. The difference between a *winner* and others is that the winner goes about in deliberate, systematic ways to continue with his development as a person.

And, awareness of Values and Goals are at the root of every worthwhile development witnessed in a person.

Areas of Personal Development can be divided into seven clear headings. As indicated before, if any developments in a specific area should affect another adversely, it could go against the basic definition of Success, which includes *useful, productive, worthwhile, and predetermined goals.*

These areas of *Personal Development* are:

1. Family Relationships
2. People Relationships
3. Career/Professional Growth
4. Money
5. Physical Well-being
6. Mind Development
7. Self-actualisation

Therefore, while engaging ourselves in a systematic Action Plan, it is most essential for each one of us to have a perfectly clear understanding of our *Values* and our *Goals*.

VALUE : A FUNCTIONAL DEFINITION

A value is something that is *freely chosen from alternatives* and is *acted upon;* something that *the individual celebrates* as being part of his creative integration in his development as a person.

As an example, let us consider and understand a simple value: *HEALTH (personal).*

To that individual to whom Health is a value in his life, he

- must have chosen it himself, after considering alternatives between being healthy and unhealthy,
- must be engaged in doing something definite to be in that state of health, and,

- must feel happy about this choice of health as a part of his value system,
- must also feel happy to speak about that value to himself as well as to others as something which he deeply cherishes.

If he realises that some of his other values might affect his health adversely, he must be ready and willing to consider those clearly, and bring about the needed changes in his own behaviour.

Has he freely chosen health as a part of his personal values?

Such persons who give advance statements like, *The doctor says that smoking is not good for my health* or *My family doesn't like it,* have not seriously accepted health as a value. Therefore, in this case, health is not a high priority of value for such a persons, or he has come to believe that his smoking habits shall not seriously affect his health.

If the value of health fulfils all the dimensions and checks of a value, only then would this person ensure that he has positive, healthy habits. Others, as you might have already noticed, will tend to act in ways that they know could be hazardous to their health. (Generally, *smokers have enough excuses for not giving up the habit, even when they do know that it has affected their health adversely.*)

Value Indicator

A Value Indicator is something which falls short of being a value.

An individual may be speaking out loud about a specific value (say, Health). But if his actions do not prove it, then it is only a Value Indicator for him.

For example, this person who says he is concerned about his health, has enough excuses to continue doing things that he says he should not do.

He will offer such excuses as, *What to do? I cannot change my habits of eating. If I eat less, I will not be able to concentrate on work.* Or, *I do want to give up smoking. But I can't. So many have tried and failed. After all, I am only a simple, ordinary man.*

In order to differentiate between a *Value* and a *Value Indicator,* we need to check them against the following *three dimensions* and *seven characteristics:*

1. Choosing
   i) Is it chosen by me freely?   Yes   No
   ii) Is it chosen by me after considering the various alternatives before me?   Yes   No
   iii) Is it chosen by me after considering the various alternatives and the consequences of each of these alternatives upon this value?   Yes   No

2. Prizing
   iv) Do I feel happy, and do I cherish having chosen this value for myself?   Yes   No
   v) Am I willing to affirm this choice of value publicly, before other people who matter to me in my life?   Yes   No

3. Doing
   vi) Am I, in actual practice, doing something in agreement with this chosen value?   Yes   No
   vii) Do I keep practising this value in various situations of my life?   Yes   No

When a person can reply *Yes* to all these seven questions, only then is the value referred to as a part of him/her.

Value Ranking

Value Ranking is a process whereby a person examines his values, as comprehensively and as thoroughly as possible, puts them within a hierarchy of values (in a list of priority showing from High to Low,) in so far as he as an individual considers it fit.

Value Ranking is a conscious, deliberate and systematic process by which a mature person arrives at a well-defined, thought-out, priority list of chosen values. He/she shall know what they want precisely and clearly.

VALUES: A PRIORITY LIST

A priority list is one prepared by an individual where he/she has shown all his/her chosen values within a specific framework of his/her life and in which each of the values are arranged in tune in their importance relative to other values. The most important value is shown at the top and the least important one, at the bottom.

Goals/Objectives

Goals or Objectives are *clearly defined end results*.
To have goals, you will need to know:
Who you are;
Where you stand now, and
What contributions you want to make in your life.

These are personal and can be assessed only by the individual himself/herself. They are action expressions of your Value system.

Writing Goals/Objectives

Writing down your objectives calls for attention to five components. A goal is understood or stated clearly only when it is complete in all the five areas.

Example

1. A preposition   : To
2. A verb   : complete
3. A subject   : the study of
4. A value   : Computer Programming
5. Time/Target statement : by June 24, 1996.

Each stated Goal must be checked against the following too:

A Check List for Objectives	Yes	Maybe	No
1. Is this objective/goal practically possible?	___	___	___
2. Is this objective/goal attainable?	___	___	___
3. Is this objective worth all the efforts that I will be required to put in?	___	___	___
4. Have I stated my goal/ objective clearly?	___	___	___
5. Have I stated my goal/ objective after considering its compatibility with my Family Relationships/ People Relationships/			

Career Growth/Money/
Physical Well-being/
Mind Development/
Self-actualisation?

Now, it is high time we got down to the actual work.

CREATING THE "MY ACTION PLAN" (MAP)

The materials that follow are divided into seven *sections*, each relating to a specific area of Personal Development.

Each of them are further divided into *two sub-sections*: Sheets A and B.

Use a pencil (so that you could easily erase a response if you feel the need to change) and continue working on each of the sections.

For example:

Section 1 is on FAMILY RELATIONSHIPS

Section 1/Sheet A : This provides a list (in alphabetical order) of the possible values in this area of development.

Read through them. Familiarise yourself with some of the values related to developing ideal Family Relationships.

Section 1/Sheet B : This contains certain important question
Value Discovery and columns for your responses. This list is not exhaustive, nor complete. As you check through the list of values, you will discover that there could be many more that you could add.

Responding to Column 3: Yes/No

Read each question in column 2, one by one, think about it and tick either *Yes* or *No* in column 3.

Very often you will be required to reflect deeply before responding to either *Yes* or *No*. In case you are not too sure, you must choose that response which will provide enough scope for possible improvements. If there is even a slight doubt or dissatisfaction, you must choose that column which shall afford an opportunity for your further growth.

Responding to Column 4: OK/Not OK

After completing column 3, consider each of your Yes/No responses (marked by you in column 3) by indicating your satisfaction or dissatisfaction.

For example, in column 3, if you had marked 'Yes', ask yourself, *Is this response/behaviour OK with me or Not OK with me?* You may now choose the appropriate response, and enter it.

In column 5 write down the *value* that *you feel* is contained within the question.

If you need some help, you may refer to sheet A where the comprehensive list of values is shown.

As you begin to fill up these columns, you will understand the proper procedure.

This workshop *should not* be considered like working on a coin-operated vending machine—drop a coin and the desired object pops up. You will need to think and decide.

A human being is not made up of a collection of buttons; a set of precisely defined, concrete factors. He/she is a universe of relationships within.

These exercises will make you think, to contemplate deep within you and make you choose what is good for you. You might even find it difficult to make a choice. But, progressively the mist will clear and the visibility will become evident. You will begin to enjoy this exercise. You will experience a feeling of discovery.

You will WIN.

Remember . . .
— There could be repetitions of values. Let it be so. These are intended to provide you with a wider range. It is possible that we could have left out quite a few important values. In such cases, you may go ahead and add them too.
— Occasionally, you could experience difficulties in making a choice between "Yes" and "No". In such cases, make a choice that is closer to reality. Your choice must also afford you ample scope for growth.
— After you have consciously arrived at the Priority of Values, the next section will show you how to proceed further.

Ready?

Here we go . . .

Section 1/Sheet A

List showing some of the Key Values in
FAMILY RELATIONSHIPS

1. Acceptance/Serenity/Tolerance
2. Accountability/Responsibility
3. Achievement/Sharing
4. Active/Involvement
5. Adaptability/Flexibility
6. Administration/Control
7. Affection
8. Appreciation
9. Approval
10. Assurance/Care
11. Attitude/Knowing/Personal
12. Being Liked
13. Belonging/Security/Togetherness
14. Comfort
15. Compassion/Care
16. Concern
17. Contribution/Education/Development/Growth/Morality/Ethics
18. Control/Order/Discipline
19. Cooperation
20. Courage
21. Courtesy
22. Criteria/Rationality
23. Decisions/Implemenation/Responsibility
24. Divinity/Nature
25. Economics/Success
26. Empathy
27. Encouragement/Individuality
28. Environment/Growth/Welcome
29. Evaluation/Positive
30. Evolution
31. Examination/Inspection
32. Expectations/Belonging
33. Expression/Freedom
34. Fairness/Encouragement
35. Fear/Personal/Environmental
36. Freedom/Acceptance/Security/Sharing
37. Happiness
38. Harmony/Systems
39. Health/Environment/Relationship
40. Honour
41. Hospitality
42. Human Dignity
43. Idealism
44. Impartiality
45. Independence
46. Influence/Neighbourhood/Positive
47. Inspiration
48. Integration/Wholeness
49. Interdependence/Whole
50. Intimacy
51. Involvement
52. Joy/Sharing
53. Justice
54. Knowing
55. Leadership
56. Learning/Education
57. Love/Expression/Respect
58. Loyalty
59. Membership/Institution
60. Mission/Goals
61. Motivation/Attitudes

62. Nurturing
63. Openness
64. Organisation
65. Participation/Decisions
66. Performance
67. Planning/System
69. Play/Leisure
70. Policy/Sharing
71. Pride/Belonging
72. Pride/Belonging
73. Principles/Adherence
74. Protection
75. Purpose/Goals
76. Realisation/Needs
77. Reassurance
78. Recreation
79. Regard
80. Rejuvenation
81. Relaxation
82. Respect/Authority
83. Responsibility
84. Role/Awareness/Action/Responsibility
85. Sacrifice
86. Savings/Authority
87. Respect/Authority
88. Self-dependence
89. Self-worth
90. Sensitivity/Feelings
91. Sharing/Listening/Trust
92. Spirituality
93. Spontaneity/Sharing
94. Strength
95. Sufficiency
96. Supportive
97. Tenacity
98. Togetherness/Sharing
99. Tolerance
100. Truthfulness
101. Understanding/Trust
102. Unity
103. Wisdom

Section 1/Sheet B

Family Relationships Values

(1) S. No.	(2) Question	(3) Yes/No	(4) OK/Not OK	(5) Value
1.	Do I feel proud and happy about my family? (*Pride/Esteem*)			
2.	When I am outside my home, am I looking forward to returning to be with my family? Do I feel the Sense of Belonging within my family unit? (*Love and Belonging*)			
3.	Are members of my family made to feel free and			

Planned Personality Development

(1) S. No.	(2) Question	(3) Yes/No	(4) OK/Not OK	(5) Value
	comfortable to share their feelings with other members of the unit? (*Sharing*)	____	____	____
4.	Is the atmosphere in our home positive to the growth and development of all members of the unit? (*Nurturing*)	____	____	____
5.	Do I feel free to invite my friends to my home, feeling confident that they will be approved and accepted by other members? (*Affection/Tolerance*)	____	____	____
6.	Are we making systematic savings for the future welfare of family members? (*Contribution/Security*)	____	____	____
7.	Do members of my family appreciate and 'stroke' each other? (*Appreciation*)	____	____	____
8.	Are family decisions/outings planned together? (*Collective Bargaining*)	____	____	____
9.	Do we have certain 'guidelines', accepted by all, establishing the rights and responsibilities of each member of the family unit? (*Role/Responsibility*)	____	____	____
10.	Do we look after our house servant/s like members of our own family unit? (*Compassion/Care*)	____	____	____

(1) S. No.	(2) Question	(3) Yes/No	(4) OK/Not OK	(5) Value
11.	Am I able to relax completely when I am back within my family unit? (*Equanimity/Peace*)			
12.	Do I often engage in hasty actions which hurt the feelings of other family members? (*Empathy*)			
13.	Am I aware of the attitudes that are developing in other members of my family? (*Awareness*)			
14.	Am I making contributions towards the education and development of other members within my family unit? (*Education/Growth/Development*)			
15.	Am I aware of the effect of the neighbourhood on the social, moral and educational development on the members of my family unit? (*External Environment*)			
16.	Do I enjoy intimacy with key members of my family unit? (*Intimacy*)			
17.	Do children in the family look forward to the homecoming of the head of the household with joyous expectations? (*Affection*)			
18.	Are junior members of the family given the chance to			

Planned Personality Development

(1) S. No.	(2) Question	(3) Yes/No	(4) OK/Not OK	(5) Value
	'think things out' for themselves? (*Freedom/Independence*)	___	___	___
19.	Have I made any provisions for my family in case sudden death strikes me? (*Protection*)	___	___	___
20.	Are arguments a source of continued unhappiness within our family unit? (*Tolerance/Support*)	___	___	___

Section 2/Sheet A

List showing some of the Key Values in PEOPLE RELATIONSHIPS

1. Acceptance
2. Accountability
3. Adaptability
4. Affection/Receiving/Giving
5. Appearance/Sobriety
6. Appreciation/Receiving/Giving
7. Assertiveness
8. Attitude/Theory Y/Theory X
9. Austerity/Behaviour
10. Belonging/Supportive
11. Centred/Self/Others
12. Charity
13. Choices/Conscious
14. Clarity/Purpose
15. Cleanliness
16. Commitment
17. Communication
18. Compassion
19. Competence/Self
20. Confidence/Self/General
21. Consistency/Truth
22. Contribution/Self/Others
23. Control/Self/People
24. Conversation Skills
25. Courtesy/Expression
26. Courtesy/Respect/Greetings
27. Curiosity/Intellectual
28. Decorum/Adaptability
29. Delightfulness
30. Detachment/Solitude
31. Development/Growth
32. Duty/Obedience/Obligations
33. Encouraging/Inspiring
34. Entertaining
35. Equanimity/Poise
36. Ethics
37. Expectations
38. Expressions/Sharing
39. Eye Contact

40. Flexibility
41. Friendless/Likeable
42. Friendship
43. Generosity
44. Get-along/Ability
45. Giving/Capacity
46. Goals/Winning
47. Gratitude
48. Guiding/Supportive
49. Helpful
50. Honesty
51. Honour
52. Hospitality
53. Humane
54. Human Dignity/ Consideration
55. Independence
56. Individuality/Steadfast
57. Influence/Being/Self
58. Interdependence
59. Inspiring/Self/Others
60. Intimacy
61. Joy/Happiness
62. Joy/Happiness
63. Judgement/ Understanding
64. Justice/Fairness
65. Leadership/Group Input
66. Likeable/Self/Others
67. Listening/Empathetic
68. Love/Affection
69. Loyalty/Respect
70. Magnanimity
71. Objectivity
72. Organisation
73. Patience
74. Persuasion/Influence
75. Perception
76. Pleasance/Cheerfulness
77. Poise/Equanimity
78. Praise/Others/Self
79. Progress
80. Punctuality
81. Purposeful
82. Recognition/Rewards
83. Regard/Consideration
84. Remembrance
85. Respect/Regard
86. Respectability
87. Responsibility
88. Richness
89. Search/Meaning
90. Selective/Choices
91. Serenity
92. Service/Attitude
93. Sharing/Listening/Trust
94. Social Affirmation/ Commitment
95. Status/Prestige
96. Supportive/Community
97. Tolerance
98. Truthfulness
99. Universality
100. Willingness to learn/ Change

Section 2/Sheet B

PEOPLE RELATIONSHIPS Values

(1) S. No.	(2) Question	(3) Yes/No	(4) OK/Not OK	(5) Value
1.	Am I generally human when I: — Speak?			

(1) S. No.	(2) Question	(3) Yes/No	(4) OK/Not OK	(5) Value
	— Write?	____	____	____
	— Shake hands or offer greetings?	____	____	____
	— Speak to juniors?	____	____	____
	— Introduce someone?	____	____	____
	— Smile?	____	____	____
	(*Courtesy*)			
2.	Do I frequently listen to people before I form an opinion of my own? (*Consideration*)	____	____	____
3.	Am I persuasive and confident before groups of people? (*Communication/Confidence*)	____	____	____
4.	Am I really interested in the things that are important to other people? (*Sharing*)	____	____	____
5.	Do I generally take up meaningful, purposeful topics for discussions in my social conversations? (*Objectivity*)	____	____	____
6.	Do I have habits that are generally disliked by the people I come across? (*Self-awareness*)	____	____	____
7.	Do I have an intellectual curiosity for knowing and understanding the convictions and beliefs of other people? (*Curiosity/Knowledge*)	____	____	____
8.	Am I easily influenced by the arguments of other people? (*Conviction*)	____	____	____

(1) S. No.	(2) Question	(3) Yes/No	(4) OK/Not OK	(5) Value
9.	Do I genuinely feel interested in the success of my friends and my business associates? (*Magnanimity*)	____	____	____
10.	Do I feel confident that I am constantly striving to improve my relationships with others? (*Progress/Growth*)	____	____	____
11.	Do I generally have the capacity to make people around me, and those I come across in the normal course of life, feel needed? (*Empathy/Care/Love*)	____	____	____
12.	Am I able to remain basically the same person when I am with different groups of people? (*Conviction/Steadfast*)	____	____	____
13.	Do I generally make a big fuss about some pettiness when I notice it in other people? (*Tolerance*)	____	____	____
14.	Can I assert my opinions clearly and confidently, without causing dimensions and harming my relationships with others? (*Assertiveness*)	____	____	____
15.	Is my appearance and manner of dress generally considered as clean, neat and acceptable to others? (*Social Conduct/Appearance*)	____	____	____

Planned Personality Development

(1) S. No.	(2) Question	(3) Yes/No	(4) OK/Not OK	(5) Value
16.	Do I actively participate in the affairs of social, civic, charitable and other fraternal organisations? (*Social concern/Contribution*)	―――	―――	―――
17.	Do I appreciate other people often and with genuine love for them? (*Appreciation/Love*)	―――	―――	―――
18.	If I am called upon to speak before a group without much advance notice, can I do it acceptably, bringing joy to others and to myself? (*Communication/Sharing*)	―――	―――	―――
19.	Do I offer help, advice, and guidance to others when they are in need of it and without expecting anything in return? (*Concern/Help*)	―――	―――	―――
20.	Am I able to know what specific social situations make me feel comfortable and why? (*Awareness/Social Values*)	―――	―――	―――

Section 3/Sheet A

List showing some of the Key Values in
CAREER DEVELOPMENT

1. Accomplishment
2. Accountability/Self/Others
3. Administration
4. Affirmation/Worth/Others

5. Aggression/Pragmatism
6. Ambition
7. Analysis/Insight
8. Appropriateness
9. Approval
10. Assessment/Self/Others
11. Attitudes
12. Capability/Aptitude
13. Capacity/Leadership
14. Choice
15. Clarity/Purpose/Goals
16. Comfort/Process
17. Communication/Non-Verbal
18. Communication/Oral/Written
19. Communication/Empathy
20. Competence
21. Consideration
22. Consultation/Assignment
23. Contribution/Skill/Knack
24. Contribution/Social
25. Creativity
26. Decision/Consultation
27. Deserve
28. Development/Awareness
29. Discussions
30. Efficiency
31. Empathy
32. Engagement/Time
33. Enjoyment/Satisfaction
34. Example/Setting/Learning
35. Excellence
36. Expectations/Awareness
37. Expectations/Pragmatism
38. Expression/Skill/Art
39. Freedom/Autonomy
40. Fulfilment
41. Happiness
42. Imagination
43. Freedom
44. Independence
45. Influence/Environment
46. Introspection
47. Knowledge/Insight/Theory
48. Management/Skills
49. Memory/Efficiency
50. Motive/Interest
51. Motivation/Others/Skills
52. Motivation/Personal
53. Objectivity/Behaviour
54. Objectives/Goals
55. Optimism
56. Orientation/Results
57. Perception
58. Planning/Goal-setting
59. Poise/Equanimity
60. Policy
61. Procedure
62. Process/Management/Grasp
63. Purposeful/Objectivity
64. Quality/Product/Standard
65. Quality/Work/Services
66. Regulation
67. Relationship/People
68. Relationship/Departmental
69. Relationship/Skills
70. Responsibility
71. Returns/Efficiency
72. Satisfaction
73. Self-employment
74. Sharing
75. Skills/Learning
76. Skills/Friendliness
77. Specialisation/Growth
78. Success
79. Trust/Freedom/Liberty
80. Understanding/Business

Planned Personality Development 163

81. Understanding/ Management
82. Understanding/Practice
83. Understanding/Synthesis
84. Understanding/Theory
85. Understanding/People
86. Understanding/Knowledge
87. Usefulness/Being
88. Utilisation/Talents/Time
89. Vision
90. Visualisation
91. Wealth/Friendship
92. Wisdom

Section 3/Sheet B
CAREER DEVELOPMENT Values

(1) S. No.	(2) Question	(3) Yes/No	(4) OK/Not OK	(5) Value
1.	Are the skills I possess sufficiently developed to do justice to my work? (*Job Skills*)	___	___	___
2.	If I am asked to write down the factors which give me a sense of satisfaction in my present career/occupation, can I do it? (*Satisfaction*)	___	___	___
3.	If I am asked to write down those factors which make me feel dissatisfied about my present career/occupation, can I do it? (*Dissatisfaction*)	___	___	___
4.	Have I been making reasonable progress in my career/occupation? (*Career Growth*)	___	___	___
5.	Can I clearly state what personal values have contributed whenever I was successful (or unsuccessful) in my career? (*Success Values*)	___	___	___

(1) S. No.	(2) Question	(3) Yes/No	(4) OK/Not OK	(5) Value
6.	Am I making conscious efforts to acquire specialised areas of knowledge to ensure my career/professional growth? (*Knowledge/Growth*)	___	___	___
7.	Am I able to discharge my responsibilities well within the time available to me? (*Time Management*)	___	___	___
8.	Are my inner dialogues generally focussed on: — Shortcomings? — Ills about the work situation? — Ills about the society? — Incompetence of superiors? — Inefficiency of others? (*Awareness/Introspection*)	___ ___ ___ ___ ___	___ ___ ___ ___ ___	___ ___ ___ ___ ___
9.	Are my expectations about the people I work with: — Generally negative? — Generally positive? — Neutral? — I don't know? — I haven't thought about it? (*Expectations*)	___ ___ ___ ___ ___	___ ___ ___ ___ ___	___ ___ ___ ___ ___
10.	Am I acting in a responsible and accountable manner in my work situations? (*Responsibility/Accountability*)	___	___	___
11.	Is my present career helping (in some ways) to achieve my future			

Planned Personality Development

(1) S. No.	(2) Question	(3) Yes/No	(4) OK/Not OK	(5) Value
	career goals? *(Career Growth)*	___	___	___
12.	Am I making some positive contributions to the society, of which I am a part, through my work? *(Contribution/Society)*	___	___	___
13.	Do I possess sufficient practical understanding of the management/ business process? *(Learning/Growth)*	___	___	___
14.	Am I making concerted efforts to clarify the precise results expected of me in my work? *(Objectivity/Awareness)*	___	___	___
15.	Do I find that projects are always thrust upon me without even consulting me first? *(Being Passive/Assertive)*	___	___	___
16.	Am I generally satisfied with the inter-departmental relationships I maintain at work? *(Career Relationships)*	___	___	___
17.	Do I feel confident that my skills of communication are sufficiently well developed? *(Communication Skills)*	___	___	___
18.	Am I in the habit of consulting my subordinates before I take decisions which could affect them and their work? *(Collective Bargaining)*	___	___	___

(1) S. No.	(2) Question	(3) Yes/No	(4) OK/Not OK	(5) Value
19.	Am I generally aware of the methods I adopt in motivating others to do the jobs? (*Attitude Motivation/Fear/Incentive*)	____	____	____
20.	Am I good at my abilities to speak with clarity and be understood by persons of different phases, culture and walks of life? (*Interpersonal Skills*)	____	____	____

Section 4/Sheet A

List showing some of the Key Values related to MONEY

1. Accountability
2. Achievement/Success/Earning
3. Accumulation/Savings
4. Adequacy/Sufficiency
5. Administration/Control
6. Assessment/Self/Capacities
7. Assistance/Support
8. Attitudes/Positive
9. Bargaining
10. Budgeting
11. Carefulness
12. Clarity/Goals
13. Commitment/Action
14. Competence
15. Confidence
16. Contentment/Wisdom
17. Courage
18. Credibility/Trustworthy
19. Criteria/Rationality
20. Dependence/Self
21. Deserving/Growth
22. Development/Growth/Worth
23. Discrimination/Wisdom
24. Duty/Obligations
25. Economics/Control/Profit
26. Economics/Success
27. Efficiency
28. End/Utilisation
29. Entertainment/Recreation
30. Equanimity
31. Expectations
32. Fairness/Justice
33. Food/Warmth/Shelter
34. Fulfilment/Obligations
35. Generosity
36. Interdependence
37. Knowledge/Insight
38. Management/Efficiency
39. Maturity
40. Objectives/Goals

41. Objectivity
42. Observation/Learning/Wisdom
43. Planning/Growth
44. Power/Authority
45. Pragmatism
46. Pride/Satisfaction
47. Priorities
48. Productivity
49. Progress
50. Promptness
51. Property/Control
52. Protection/Assurance
53. Reality/Awareness
54. Relaxation/Enjoyment
55. Reliance/Self
56. Responsibility
57. Returns
58. Satisfaction/Needs
59. Savings
60. Security
61. Sharing/Giving
62. Solutions
63. Utilisation

Section 4/Sheet B

MONEY Values

(1) S. No.	(2) Question	(3) Yes/No	(4) OK/Not OK	(5) Value
1.	Do I feel that I know how to use money productively? (*Productivity*)	____	____	____
2.	Do I engaged in systematic planning of financial development in my life? (*Management/Development*)	____	____	____
3.	Do I believe in setting, and acting within 'operating budgets'? (*Budgeting/Controlling*)	____	____	____
4.	Have my earnings increased at a satisfactory pace during the past five years? (*Growth/Financial*)	____	____	____
5.	Is wise buying and spending a total concern within my family? (*Collective Wisdom*)	____	____	____

(1) S. No.	(2) Question	(3) Yes/No	(4) OK/Not OK	(5) Value
6.	Do I intelligently observe how other people in my income bracket, manage to put their finances to more productive uses? (*Personal Wisdom/ Observation*)	____	____	____
7.	Do I feel justly proud of the material comforts I provide to myself and to my family members? (*Objectivity*)	____	____	____
8.	Am I overtaxing myself to earn money even at the cost of things I cherish doing? (*Self-sufficiency*)	____	____	____
9.	Can I pay other people fairly for the work done, promptly and without much cribbing? (*Fair Dealings*)	____	____	____
10.	Am I careful with others' money as I am with mine? (*Attitude*)	____	____	____
11.	Do I often engage in gambling with money as a primary source of entertainment? (*Responsibility/Using Money*)	____	____	____
12.	Do I pay my bills promptly and on due dates? (*Promptness/Concern for others*)	____	____	____
13.	Could I meet my financial obligations if I were unable to work			

(1) S. No.	(2) Question	(3) Yes/No	(4) OK/Not OK	(5) Value
	for a six-month period? (*Savings/Future Provisions*)	____	____	____
14.	Am I doing anything concrete to increase my worth, and thus add to my financial income? (*Planning/Growth*)	____	____	____
15.	Am I capable of living happily within my financial income? (*Wisdom/Pragmatism*)	____	____	____
16.	Do I often put a high stress on bargaining before parting with my money? (*Tightfisted/Bargains*)	____	____	____
17.	Do I often feel that with more money, all my financial problems shall disappear? (*Wisdom*)	____	____	____
18.	Am I often tempted to buy things and accumulate them? (*Security*)	____	____	____

Section 5/Sheet A

Sheet showing some of the Key Values related to PHYSICAL WELL-BEING

1. Acceptance
2. Achievement/Success
3. Activity
4. Adaptability/Flexibility
5. Atonement
6. Attitude/Positive
7. Autonomy
8. Awe/Wonder/Curiosity
9. Cheerfulness
10. Competence
11. Consciousness/Awareness
12. Consistency
13. Construction/New Order
14. Control/Exercise/Order
15. Control/Discipline
16. Criteria/Rationality
17. Decision-making

18. Detachment
19. Diet/Balance/Nutrition
20. Discovery/Delight
21. Energy
22. Enjoyment/Pleasure
23. Equilibrium/Health
24. Experience
25. Expressive/Freedom
26. Fitness/System
27. Freedom/Will
28. Food/Habit/Nutrition
29. Function
30. Growth/Expansion
31. Habits/Formation
32. Harmony
33. Health/Personal
34. Imagination
35. Integration/Wholeness
36. Intelligence/Application
37. Maintenance
38. Medicine
39. Membership/Institution
40. Nourishment
41. Objectivity
42. Observation/Self
43. Participation/Activity
44. Play/Leisure
45. Priorities
46. Productivity
47. Psychosomatic
48. Recreation/Free Sense
49. Regularity
50. Relationship/Consultant Help
51. Relaxation
52. Repair/Maintenance
53. Response
54. Responsibility/Management
55. Rest
56. Retention
57. Safety/Security
58. Safety/Survival
59. Sanitation/Hygiene
60. Search/Meaning
61. Security/Safety
62. Self-competence/Confidence
63. Self-control
64. Self-direction
65. Self-worth
66. Serenity/Peace
67. Tolerance
68. Truth/Wisdom/Insight
69. Understanding/Knowledge
70. Vacation/Recreation
71. Well-being
72. Work/Labour
73. Workmanship/Craft
74. Yoga

Section 5/Sheet B

PHYSICAL WELL-BEING

(1) S. No.	(2) Question	(3) Yes/No	(4) OK/Not OK	(5) Value
1.	Are my habits generally consistent with maintaining good health? (*Habits*)	____	____	____

Planned Personality Development

(1) S. No.	(2) Question	(3) Yes/No	(4) OK/Not OK	(5) Value
2.	Am I addicted to anything, without which I just cannot go on with my normal working and living? (*Addiction*)	___	___	___
3.	Can I fast completely for 24 hours without much physical and emotional strain? (*Leadership/Self-control*)	___	___	___
4.	Do I often engage in improving my awareness and understanding necessary for continual development of physical health and well-being? (*Insight/Knowledge/Learning*)	___	___	___
5.	Do I know how to relax completely? (*Relaxation*)	___	___	___
6.	Do I often willingly engage in conversations about my illness and deprivations? — Do I often willingly engage in conversations about good health and enrichments? (*Attitudes*)	___	___	___
7.	Do I know what 'Psychosomatic Diseases' are? (*Body/Mind Link*)	___	___	___
8.	Do I get as much physical exercise as I need to keep myself in good working condition? (*Maintenance*)	___	___	___

(1) S. No.	(2) Question	(3) Yes/No	(4) OK/Not OK	(5) Value
9.	Do I generally get carried away by the advice of others about good health? (*Conviction*)	____	____	____
10.	Do I feel that I am competent enough to take charge of myself and am able to work towards my growth and physical well-being? (*Self-direction*)	____	____	____
11.	Are my attitudes towards my own health in the best, long-range interests of my family? (*Concern/Others*)	____	____	____
12.	Do I generally have well-informed views about major health hazards that people seem to suffer from all over? (*Awareness/Knowledge*)	____	____	____
13.	Am I a slave to my tongue, to the extent that I cannot relish any other foods than those which I have special liking for? (*Addiction/Conditioning*)	____	____	____
14.	Do I know how to respond intelligently to the various reactions of my body at different times? (*Self/Body Awareness*)	____	____	____
15.	During holidays, am I generally able to detach myself from my career-related work completely? (*Detachment/Relaxation*)	____	____	____

(1) S. No.	(2) Question	(3) Yes/No	(4) OK/Not OK	(5) Value
16.	When I visit a sick friend in hospital, am I generally conscious about the topics I should discuss and those I should avoid? (*Awareness/Concern*)	____	____	____
17.	Have I ever wondered at the complex mechanism that the body is, and how it continues to function silently and efficiently? (*Awe/Wonder/Curiosity*)	____	____	____
18.	Do I have any explanations as to how and why so many people, who live in the dirtiest slums, are healthy and strong? (*Realisation/Truth*)	____	____	____
19.	Do I know how to relax every part of my body consciously, progressively and systematically? (*Relaxation/Awareness*)	____	____	____
20.	Do I enjoy long walks? (*Awareness/Exercise*)	____	____	____

Section 6/Sheet A

List showing some of the key values related to MIND DEVELOPMENT

1. Acceptance
2. Accomplishment
3. Achievement/Success
4. Accountability/Self
5. Adaptability/Flexible
6. Adequacy
7. Alertness
8. Analysis/Organisation
9. Aspiration/Achievement
10. Assertion/Self
11. Attitudes
12. Being/Self
13. Capacity/Self
14. Confidence/Self
15. Construction/New Order

16. Contemplation/Asceticism
17. Control/Discipline/Order
18. Conversation/Self-awareness
19. Courage
20. Courtesy/Respect
21. Creativity/Ideation
22. Criteria/Rationality
23. Culture/Developmen
24. Curiosity/Sensitivity
25. Dependence
26. Detachment/Solitude
27. Determination/Firmness
28. Dignity
29. Discovery/Delight
30. Education/Certification
31. Education/Insight
32. Efficiency
33. Equilibrium/Poise
34. Expansion/Self
35. Expectations
36. Exploration/Search
37. Expressiveness/Freedom
38. Evaluation/Self Systems
39. Faith/Beliefs
40. Fantasy/Play
41. Foresight
42. Formation/Habits
43. Functioning
44. Growth/Expansion
45. Harmony/Systems
46. Honour
47. Imagination
48. Independence
49. Initiative
50. Intellect/Curiosity
51. Intimacy/Solitude
52. Interdependence
53. Invention/Creativity
54. Laws/Guide
55. Learning/Curiosity
56. Learning/Understand/Skill
57. Listening/Understanding
58. Management/Self
59. Memory Efficiency
60. Mission/Goals
61. Modes/Alternatives
62. Objectivity
63. Observation/Insight
64. Patriotism/Esteem
65. Pioneering/Invention
66. Planning
67. Planning/Future Growth
68. Points of View/Alternatives
69. Poise/Control
70. Power/Authority
71. Pragmatism
72. Productivity
73. Pursuit/Excellence
74. Reading/Purposeful
75. Reading/Comprehension
76. Recreation/Free Sense
77. Relaxation
78. Research/Openness
79. Resolution/Firmness
80. Responsibility
81. Richness
82. Reliance/Self
83. Self-centred
84. Self-confidence/Competence
85. Self-control
86. Self/Delight/Joyful
87. Simplicity/Playfulness
88. Sleep/Rejuvenation
89. Solutions/Alternatives

Planned Personality Development

90. Supplement/Refreshment
91. Synthesis/Relate
92. Talents/Utilisation
93. Training/Development
94. Truth/Wisdom/Insight
95. Trust/Self
96. Visualisation
97. Vitality/Freshness

Section 6/Sheet B

MIND DEVELOPMENT Values

(1) S. No.	(2) Question	(3) Yes/No	(4) OK/Not OK	(5) Value
1.	Do I still feel the spirit of exploration and adventure as I felt as a child? *(Spontaneity)*			
2.	Do I rate myself high in my abilities to form relationships, to connect current events and their ultimate effects on myself and my career/profession/business? *(Observation/Insight)*			
3.	Do I enjoy the process of wide and varied reading? *(Curiosity/Learning/Knowing)*			
4.	Do I often talk as if I am of 'average' or 'poor' capacity *(Self-image)*			
5.	Do I allot time for and engage myself in cultural and mental development? *(Expansion/Mind)*			
6.	Am I generally well-informed about the environment, events and people? *(Perspectives)*			

(1) S. No.	(2) Question	(3) Yes/No	(4) OK/Not OK	(5) Value
7.	Do I strive to use my imagination and inventive powers to solve problems that I come across in day-to-day living? (*Resources/Synthesis*)	___	___	___
8.	Do I generally feel the sense of accomplishment, well-being and purpose within me? (*Self-sufficiency*)	___	___	___
9.	Am I generally very enthusiastic about all the activities that I am responsible for? (*Enthusiasm/Zest*)	___	___	___
10.	Can I keep myself usefully engaged and happy if I have to remain alone for long periods of time? (*Serenity*)	___	___	___
11.	Do I consider my learning rate to be fast and deep enough? (*Learning/Comprehension*)	___	___	___
12.	Do I often blame 'other people' to cover up my shortcomings? (*Self-image*)	___	___	___
13.	Do I often consciously analyse my thoughts deeply and organise them towards achieving worthy goals? (*Analysis/Re-organisation*)	___	___	___

(1) S. No.	(2) Question	(3) Yes/No	(4) OK/Not OK	(5) Value
14.	Do I feel that without a cup of tea or a cigarette or some such other thing, my day cannot begin? (*Addiction/Self-control*)	_____	_____	_____
15.	Can I habitually think of more alternate solutions to problems than merely just one? (*Pragmatism/Alternatives*)	_____	_____	_____
16.	Do I sometimes feel that I should recapture the vitality, freshness and the sense of wonder I used to feel when I was younger? (*Youth/Vitality/Conditioning*)	_____	_____	_____
17.	Am I addicted to any form of negative mental conditioning such as:			
	— "What will other people think of me?"	_____	_____	_____
	— "It is too late to do anything now..."	_____	_____	_____
	— "There is no point in trying now. I know it will not work. So many have already failed." (*Hopeful vs Hopelessness*)	_____	_____	_____
18.	Do I sleep well? (*Sleep/Relaxation*)	_____	_____	_____
19.	Can I, and do I, generally accept responsibility for my failures without offering unwanted excuses? (*Accountability/Acceptance*)	_____	_____	_____

(1) S. No.	(2) Question	(3) Yes/No	(4) OK/Not OK	(5) Value
20.	Do I feel very strongly about certain types of food, to the extent that I do not even try something new or different? (*Openness/Pragmatism*)			

Section 7/Sheet A
List showing some of the Key Values in SELF-ACTUALISATION

1. Acceptance
2. Adequacy
3. Admiration/Wonder
4. Affection/Love
5. Alive
6. Art/Beauty
7. Attainment/Success
8. Attainment/Success
9. Austerity/Lack of Greed
10. Awakening
11. Celebration
12. Change/Progress
13. Charity
14. Compassion/Love
15. Completion
16. Concentration
17. Concepts
18. Concern
19. Conduct (Self)
20. Congruence
21. Contemplation
22. Contribution
23. Conviction
24. Creation/Invention
25. Credibility
26. Deserving
27. Destiny
28. Detachment
29. Development/Ethics
30. Discovery/Delight
31. Divinity
32. Ecstasy/Beauty/Aesthetics
33. Effortlessness
34. Equanimity/Poise
35. Ethics/Empathy
36. Excellence
37. Faith/Belief
38. Freedom/Expressiveness
39. Genuineness
40. Giving/Sharing
41. Goal/Ultimate
42. God
43. God/Personal Equation
44. Goodness
45. Honesty/Truthfulness
46. Honour
47. Humility
48. Individuality
49. Ingenuity
50. Influence/Community
51. Inquiry
52. Intuitive Insight
53. Joy/Serenity/Happiness

54. Justice
55. Law/Principles/Guide
56. Liberation
57. Life/Self-actualisation
58. Meaningfulness
59. Meditation
60. Membership/Institution
61. Morality
62. Nature
63. Obedience
64. Order
65. Perfection
66. Philosophy
67. Playfulness
68. Points of view
69. Prayer
70. Pride/Deserving
71. Principles/Laws
72. Purpose
73. Reading/Wisdom
74. Realisation (Self)
75. Religion
76. Responsibility (Social)
77. Richness
78. Rituals/Practices
79. Search/Discovery/Meaning
80. Secularism
81. Self/Delight
82. Self-sufficiency
83. Serenity/Peace
84. Service/Vocation
85. Spiritual Code
86. Supportive/Society
87. Surrender
88. Sympathy
89. Synergy
90. Tolerance
91. Traditions/Culture
92. Transcendence/Global
93. Trustworthiness
94. Truth
95. Universality
96. Unlimited
97. Wisdom
98. Wonder/Awe/Curiosity
99. Wonder/Nature
100. Zest

Section 7/Sheet B
SELF-ACTUALISATION

(1) S. No.	(2) Question	(3) Yes/No	(4) OK/Not OK	(5) Value
1.	Do I feel a moral responsibility to develop and utilise my talents for the common good? (*Contribution*)	___	___	___
2.	Do I consciously seek to find out the values behind the rules I live by? (*Discovery*)	___	___	___

(1) S. No.	(2) Question	(3) Yes/No	(4) OK/Not OK	(5) Value
3.	Do I enjoy the serenity and peace of mind to face any challenges life may pose for me? (*Acceptance*)	___	___	___
4.	Do I feel a deep sense of joy in keeping things in proper order? (*Orderliness*)	___	___	___
5.	Can I discuss my beliefs without ever having to become defensive about them? (*Freedom from guilt*)	___	___	___
6.	Do I often feel that I am engaged in the pursuit of excellence? (*Pursuit of Excellence*)	___	___	___
7.	Do I treat my personal servants with fairness and compassion? (*Fairness and Compassion*)	___	___	___
8.	Am I generally known as a person who shall remain committed to his words and promises? (*Credibility*)	___	___	___
9.	Do I impart to my children ethical, moral and spiritual codes and training? (*Development/Others*)	___	___	___

(1) S. No.	(2) Question	(3) Yes/No	(4) OK/Not OK	(5) Value
10.	Do I meditate? (*Meditation/Introspection*)	___	___	___
11.	Am I generally creative and imaginative? (*Creativity*)	___	___	___
12.	Is it possible to succeed and be happy in this world by practising truth? (*Truthfulness*)	___	___	___
13.	Do I feel embarrassed to speak to the poor man on the street? (*Humility/Concern/Care*)	___	___	___
14.	Am I motivated by luck, charms, or any other 'wishful' beliefs other than dedicated hard work? (*Dedication vs Escapism*)	___	___	___
15.	Do I ever feel in a moral or spiritual way that I am responsible for the welfare and happiness of others in the society? (*Social Contributions*)	___	___	___
16.	Can I love a poor, racially downtrodden person as much as my kith and kin? (*Universality*)	___	___	___
17.	Do I engage in and enjoy the process of meditating? (*Peace*)	___	___	___

(1) S. No.	(2) Question	(3) Yes/No	(4) OK/Not OK	(5) Value
18.	Do I generally understand the principles behind my spiritual beliefs? (*Meaningfulness*)	___	___	___
19.	Do I experience and enjoy a certain degree of effortlessness in living? (*Effortlessness*)	___	___	___
20.	If I am asked to define 'beauty' in a deeper sense, can I do it well alongwith some examples? (*Beauty*)	___	___	___

Section 1 to 7—Sheet C: Value Ranking

(Deliberation and Ranking of Values discovered in Column 5 of Sheet B)

Action Procedure

1. Prepare a separate sheet of paper for each of the seven areas, shown, and mark the following columns.
2. Enter all those values that you will need to work on, below each specific section.
3. Mark their relative priority against the 5 columns.

S. No.	Description of Value (Already identified in the Sheets B)	Personal Preference Scale of this Value to Me.				
		1 Very High	2 High	3 So-so	4 Below Par	5 Weak
	Family Relationships					
	People Relationships					

Planned Personality Development

S. No.	Description of Value (Already identified in the Sheets B)	Personal Preference Scale of this Value to Me.				
		1 Very High	2 High	3 So-so	4 Below Par	5 Weak
	Career Growth					
	Money					
	Physical Well-being					
	Mind Development					
	Self-actualisation					

Sheet D: Action Procedures

After studying each of the values and their relative priorities, respond by acting on each of the values through the step-by-step procedure indicated below:

1. Description of Value

2. Define Goals (What do I want to accomplish/achieve?)

3. What are the obstacles and road blocks? (What's between me and my goals?)

4. How can I overcome these obstacles? (Action Plans)

5. What am I actually going to do? (Decision)
   _____

6. What are the rewards I get when I achieve this goal?
   _____
   _____
   _____

7. Are these rewards really worthwhile to me?   YES   NO
   Enter any specific reactions you may have. _____
   _____

8. Target date for achieving this goal. _____

9. Space for any specific thoughts/ideas you may have for working on/attaining the above.
   _____
   _____
   _____
   _____
   _____

27

Skills Inventory

> "Thought asks too much and words tell too much; because to ask anything is to ask everything, and to say anything is to ask more. It is the radical defect of thought that it leaves us discontented with what we actually feel—with what we know and do not know—as we know sunlight and surfeit and terror, at once perhaps, and yet know nothing of them."
>
> R.P. BLACKMUIR
> American critic

When we were born, we did not know most of the things that we came to learn later in life. The learning process began from that moment of birth. Based on the environment, experiences, people around us, and various influences, we became the individuals that we are today. Yet, each of us have diverse aspects and are unique too.

When you and I were born, we did not know even the basic skills needed for living. We did not know how to coordinate our fingers, we did not know how to sit, how to stand, how to walk, how to run and so many other skills that have become the essential part of our lives today. We were also taught many other skills in the process of growing up.

And, have you ever wondered how enormous were the skills that we came to acquire in later years? We did not even know how to hold on to the cradle, while the mother was swinging it to put us to sleep. We did not know how to pick up objects or to use our hands. As little children, as toddlers, we learned many skills within a short span of time.

Progressively, we learned and developed many more personal skills. Walking, talking, running, cleaning . . . riding a bicycle, climbing a ladder or a tree, finding our way to the school and back.

In our schools, we were taught how to do arithmetic, use a standard language, what answers we must give to the questions that the teacher will ask of us on history, geography, science, civics, and so on. As we progressed to higher levels of formal education, the topics became wider, and the details too.

All the skills developed through all this learning can be grouped and termed together as *INSTRUMENTAL SKILLS*.

When someone learned to write on paper using a pencil, the real work was accomplished not by the pencil, or by the hand, but by the brain of the writer. The pencil or the hand was only an instrument. When you learned to play on a guitar, it was you who knew how to do it. Your hand, your body and so many other components became your instruments. Because you had acquired those skills of coordinating them, you could play.

Beyond the scope of formal education, we learned many other skills too. It might have begun with telling the mother that 'I am hungry', or preventing the elder brother from beating me, or making the shopkeeper give me that specific 'toffee' whose name I did not know. Then on, how to play with other kids, how to make compromises, how to find our way to the church or temple, how to go to the market and buy what we need, how to deal with people and the world in general. Even in the schools, we learned many personal skills which were not a part of the teaching or the examination curriculum. We had to learn them. Survival demanded that we acquire those skills.

All these skills we just discussed, relate to creating responses in others. Thus this set of skills is called *INTERPERSONAL SKILLS*.

These two are the essential, basic skills. The Instrumental Skills contribute to the extension of the individual Self. And, the

Skills Inventory

Interpersonal Skills contribute to the ways of getting along with people in general.

Most formal academic education, generally provide only skills related to the first kind. Grammar, Composition, Science, History, Geography, Mathematics, Economics, Engineering, Architecture and all the others, with minor exceptions, relate to increasing our instrumental Skills only.

The Interpersonal Skills acquired by us, came mostly through informal education. Dealing with people in the home, in the neighbourhood, meeting people in the society at large, during picnics, outings, camps, during games and through so many other interaction, we learned some of our interpersonal skills. Whenever we were placed in situations where we had to get work done through others, we had no other option than to utilise these skills.

Where the parents were more concerned about the numbers indicated in the progress report, the scores gained by the wards, and not how they were accomplished, allowed us very little opportunity for training and development in Interpersonal Skills. Often we learned how to offer *excuses* and *convince others that the failure was due to someone other than ourselves*.

During the course of our research, I have often questioned thousands of people in India on their views about these two areas of Skills Development. The general responses indicated by them, give us a clue about what exists in reality and what is truly desired.

Question : *How much of the formal education you received before entering a profession, the business or the industry, could be divided among the Instrumental and the Interpersonal Skills?*

Answer : *Instrumental*: 90 per cent.
Interpersonal: 10 per cent.

Question : *When a young person begins his/her career with a certain degree of supervisory responsibilities* (except where the skills involved were purely instrumental such as a fitter, a turner, a clerk, or an operator) *how much of the work that he/she is responsible for comes under the Instrumental and the Interpersonal Skills?*

Answer : *Interpersonal*: 90 per cent.
Instrumental: 10 per cent.

In this altered situation:

a) The new supervisor's Interpersonal Skills became very limited, and
b) The supervisory or junior management tasks brought a great deal of 'responsibilities for getting results through other people.'

Often, the others referred to possessed highly developed Instrumental Skills in their own specific areas of work.

Even those who chose to enter the sales profession found that most of their work involved dealing with people.

It would be profitable for us to examine this example a little further. This graduate engineer, during his formal education, was taught much about the engineering sciences and extended his personal knowledge of the work and its technicalities. He learned much about the theories, the laws and the concepts. But he did not learn much about those people who were engaged in such specific actions to earn their livelihood.

Now this freshly qualified engineer gets employed as a supervisor on the shop floor in an engineering industry. From day one he discovers that his present moments during work are filled with the tension of getting others to work. Most of the persons working under him were far better skilled in their specific activities. In fact, a carpenter, or a fitter, or a painter knew his job far better than the supervisor himself. But, all the same, the supervisor became responsible for getting them to work, to make them put forth their best efforts, to lead them and to achieve the targets laid down by his management. The engineer had to learn a lot more. And, if he was to survive, he knew he had better acquire those skills faster too.

Those who had thought that education was only related to Engineering and the Drawings, got hopelessly pushed around. Most of their Instrumental Skills became hardly worth anything within the career responsibilities. For survival and growth, they were forced to develop more Interpersonal Skills.

It is often said that whenever a person joins a business organisation in a supervisory or junior managerial capacity, his beginning is made possible due to his specialisation. But if he has to grow in the industry, he must learn to be a generalist

Skills Inventory

through a wider understanding of all the other areas of business and management.

The management itself, in any organisation, is classified into three levels: *Junior, Middle and Top*. The responsibilities of a Junior Manager are functionally related to his Instrumental and Interpersonal Skills. He will be effective in his work only when a balanced understanding of both Instrumental and Interpersonal Skills—50 per cent each—are developed within.

Let us make a closer scrutiny of these two skills. Think and reflect deeply, before you assess your skills. It will certainly help you in the long run if you are sincere and critical with yourself.

INSTRUMENTAL SKILLS

Instrumental Skills consist of the specific *blend of intelligence and personal efficiency* that helps an individual to become *professional and competent*. It is the skill to manipulate our ideas and the immediate environment. The skill of handicrafts, physical actions, and academic attainments come under these skills.

Some of the areas you could consider are presented below in a checklist format. We have also provided explanations below of some of the items mentioned, so that you can make your responses deeper and more pragmatic.

	OK	Not OK
1. Reading Skills. (Before you are inclined to tick off OK, please consider Reading as the *process of using your Eyes, Senses, Brain and the Mind to understand the Meanings, both Literal and the Hidden.* Most people can benefit greatly by improving their reading skills. Reading skills are not well developed by merely knowing how to understand the literal meanings that are contained in a newspaper or in the popular works of fiction. Good reading must relate to a wider range.)	_____	_____

2. Writing Skills.
   (These skills are essential for most of us to fulfil Personal, Business and Technical needs. There are of course a wider range of writing skills involved as in creating Poetry, Fiction, Literature, etc. which may not be essential for most of us.)
3. Arithmetic Skills.
   (In an emergency, without using the electronic calculators)
4. To be able to think logically.
5. To be able to coordinate the Physical Self.
   (Like driving a car, ride a bike, swimming, etc.)
6. To master New Skills in one's profession.
   (Like accounting, filing tax returns, etc.)
7. Remembering and following the procedures to be followed at work.
   (Memory Efficiency)
8. Being competent in the efforts expended (Being efficient)
9. Being able to understand technical data and apply them to logical, productive uses.
   (Read a Balance Sheet, invest money wisely, etc.)
10. To be able to generate certain results within a specified time.
    (Achieve competence in your labour)
11. To be able to achieve certain specific results using a specified amount of money (Cost-effectiveness)
12. To be able to diet, exercise, and maintain good health.
13. Form new habits and alter old ones.
14. Create certain plans of action and be able to follow them.
15. Be able to relax, meditate and acquire serenity within.

Skills Inventory

INTERPERSONAL SKILLS

Those skills that help you to deal with others with empathy, understanding and generosity which comes from a clear knowledge of oneself, are interpersonal. These are the skills of being objective and pragmatic in your own feelings, so that you gain cooperation from others, and, therefore, reduce the chances of isolation within the social set-up. Again, these skills shall help you to lead people who have come together with a common purpose.

Some of the skills that could be listed under Interpersonal Skills are:

	OK	Not OK
1. Ability to feel, and understand emotions.	___	___
2. Ability to recognise my own feelings accurately.	___	___
3. Ability to identify another's feelings accurately.	___	___
4. Sharing emotions and feelings with people.	___	___
5. Ability to express the feelings of anger objectively.	___	___
6. Ability to put myself in the 'shoes' of others and be able to experience the other's world. (Being empathetic.)	___	___
7. Objectify my own, as well as others' feelings and make others accountable.	___	___
8. Be able to clarify and communicate personal goals/objectives.	___	___
9. Remain calm, cool and poised during high stress and anxiety situations.	___	___
10. Be able to appreciate and affirm the worth of others so that they listen to you and you are able to communicate with them.	___	___
11. Ability to make yourself understood with the awareness of the skills involved. (Communication)	___	___
12. The ability and the skills to listen to the meanings as well as the feelings.	___	___

13. Enable others to see themselves through your presence.
    (Be able to create empathy in others.) _____ _____
14. Project your imagination into another's world and make it understood by them. _____ _____
15. Be present with others during moments of their personal grief.
    (During deaths, failures, etc.) _____ _____
16. Be creatively aggressive.
    (Being able to assert yourself; fighting to win and not losing people, etc.) _____ _____
17. Be able to cope with conflict and to resolve them purposefully. _____ _____
18. Discover strengths of people and organise those towards better results. _____ _____

Isn't it high time for you, and for me too, to consider the process of developing the essential skills that are needed for leading a purposeful life?

LEVELS OF SKILLS AND THEIR INTEGRATION

Basically there are four skills, and their integration comes in three different levels.

1. Instrumental Skills
2. Interpersonal Skills
3. Imaginal Skills
4. Systems Skills

Performing those professional activities which do not demand supervisory responsibilities, we can generally manage our jobs with our Instrumental Skills. But, when we consider that most of our living and walking hours are filled by interactions with people, it becomes essential for us to develop a good degree of Interpersonal Skills too.

Wherever there are leadership/supervisory/management responsibilities, they come in three different levels too: *Junior, Middle and Senior.*

If we outline these skills and levels it could appear as shown on next page:

Skills Inventory

Let us briefly discuss the other two skills too. This could help you to identify your future goals.

Imaginal Skills

That particular synthesis of imagination, fantasy and feelings that enables an individual to clarify ideas, and be able to project them in an effective and practical manner is the imaginal skill. It consists of the ability to study and make sense out of an ever-increasing amount of information. These skills demand the capacity to learn from direct experience, to choose and act on complicated alternatives. They call for creativity and purposefulness.

In Personal Development, Imaginal Skills integrate the other two skills discussed earlier.

Some of the skills that could be checked in this area are:

	OK	Not OK
1. Be able to arrive consciously at one's priority of values.		
2. Be able to gather new facts and synthesize them within the existing understanding.		
3. Be able to arrive at new arrive at new understanding from seemingly unrelated data.		
4. Perceive and clarify hidden meanings among the standard information available.		
5. Be able to imagine, and plan new and practical projects.		
6. Be able to generate and develop new skills:		
i) Getting a group to contribute towards total results.		

ii) Using the professional expertise available within or outside the system.	____	____
iii) Brain storming techniques.	____	____
iv) Creativity techniques.	____	____
7. Develop the ability and awareness to use several modes of communication.	____	____

During the final stage of Career Development come the skills that we would like to call the System Skills. These skills are essential for those who are at the top levels of Business, Industry, Government and other organisations.

System Skills

These skills are that specific combination of imagination, common sense, risk-taking and efficiency by which the individual is able to see all parts of a system of administration as it is related to the whole. They consist of the ability to plan, design and execute changes in the system, institutions, societies and other organisations, so as to allow maximum growth for each individual part. Acquiring System Skills calls for the integration of all the three skills of Career Development.

Some of the skills that could be listed under this heading are:

	OK	Not OK
1. Using money to generate money and create wealth.	____	____
2. Be able to work comfortably with various processes.	____	____
3. Be able to identify interpersonal needs and the needs of the organisation when faced with small group coordination.	____	____
4. Be able to lead complex groups towards organisational objectives.	____	____
5. Be able to synthesize complex information, statements and emotional inputs of people.	____	____

Skills Inventory

6. Be able to absorb pressures from organisational affairs and needs of the society.	_____ _____
7. Be able to speak with clarity, and be understood by persons of different phases, cultures and walks of life.	_____ _____
8. Be able to engage in long-term planning and goal-setting.	_____ _____
9. Be able to make sense and reflect meaningfully on apparently confusing information.	_____ _____
10. To be able to set down specified, clear and pragmatic organisational and individual objectives.	_____ _____

CAREER DEVELOPMENT: A STRATEGY

To the person who is happy and contented with whatever he is doing now, the question of Planned Career Development does not arise. To those millions who feel committed towards growth, the development phases identified among the four skills must be understood and mastered.

28

Attitudinal Changes

> 'The moment the slave resolves that he will no longer be a slave, his fetters fall. He frees himself and shows the way to others. Freedom and slavery are mental states."
>
> MAHATMA GANDHI
> Father of the Indian nation

L et us visualise a water storage tank located on top of one of our buildings.

The engineer who designed and fitted it, kept both the inlet and the outlet at the same level, right at the top. The water being pumped into it had been muddy and full of muck.

Attitudinal Changes

No one bothered to ensure that the supply of water was clear, clean and hygienic. Now, after a long, long period of time, a considerable amount of sludge has accumulated within the tank. In fact, this tank cannot store any more water. You see, the designer fitted both the inlets and outlets exactly at the same level at the top end. And, below that level the entire space is filled with solid sediments. The tank is no more useful for storing any water.

What shall we do now to remedy this situation?

Think. Do some brain storming.

— Open the top cover of the tank, go inside, remove all the muck?
— Cut a drain-hole at the bottom, pull out all the muck and clean it up?
— Add some chemicals, loosen the muck and drain them out?
— Blast the damn tank and fit a fresh one?

There could be a large number of approaches to solve this problem. But, if you are willing to consider this tank to be a *Human Being*, then what shall we do?

What collected in it was muck, filth and dirt. Now the inner tank is full of slime and sludge. What do we do now?

Is there a manhole through which we could go inside that person, clean all the muck and fill him up with fresh new, positive attitudes?

In a physical sense, the answer is No. However, in a practical sense, the answer is Yes. It is possible.

In discovering the answer, we shall need to look into our Habits and Attitudes.

Habits are specific methods we have developed for meeting the challenges of life. Everyday, we meet many situations that require conscious decisions and choices. Each time, we faced something, the 'brain' stored the reactions and decisions we made for future use. Once stored, it is used over and over again automatically.

Habits have their origin in consciously made decisions. And, they include both *Attitudes* and Actions.

An *Attitude* is an enduring inclination to react in a certain way each time we respond to the given situation. Thus, attitudes are habits of thought and emotional responses to a given stimulus.

CHANGING HABITS AND ATTITUDES

How can our habits and attitudes be broken or changed? It can be accomplished through a three-step process:

First : We must recognise that the habits and attitudes are our methods for *achieving some sort of satisfaction*.

Second : We must realise what *specific satisfaction* a particular habit gives us.

Third : We must substitute a more *effective habit* in place of the undesirable one.

Let us say that you have a habit that you would like to change. It may not be bad at all, but all the same you would like to change it. Any such changes within a person must come from internal acceptance and understanding. Insight is essential before any change is possible.

Earlier, we had discussed the deterring effects that conditioning could have on a person's pursuit of success. We also saw how a large number of habits and attitudes have been conditioned by our environment and associations.

Therefore, any worthwhile changes must come from an internal understanding and acceptance.

AFFIRMATIONS AND REINFORCEMENT

Affirmations to us should mean *Positive declarations of what we believe, or have come to believe to be true; that truth we believe in and desire to live by.* Quotations, Oaths, Creeds, Axioms are all affirmations.

When we say, "God is great, and His will shall prevail," it is a positive affirmation. It helps us to believe in something. It gives us a foundation to act upon.

"I am no good. I can't achieve anything worthwhile" too is an affirmation, but a negative one.

"The world is a beautiful place to live in. Everything happens in tune with Nature's Laws" is another positive affirmation.

"What you sow, you shall reap" is another.

Use of affirmations as a vehicle for personal development is one of the oldest practices of human beings.

When we practise affirmations, the laws of reinforcement begin to work for us. We start looking for those strengths and changes we have associated with our affirmations. We also begin to act like the person we have resolved to be. We literally become changed personalities.

REPETITION AND DISPLACEMENT

Most of us have practised affirmations for years. Some of them were positive and constructive ones. And, many of them were negative and destructive too.

Affirmations work according to the law of displacement. When you continue to feed a positive thought into your unconscious mind, you will displace a negative thought.

When you continue to pump fresh, clean water forcefully into the tank it will certainly begin to displace the murky, filthy water from within it. It might take time, but the dirt shall certainly get displaced.

As you continue with positive affirmations, gradually the negative attitudes—fear, doubt, worry, indecision—will get displaced.

As you continue to remain engaged in these, it will progressively bring different responses from within you.

This is how it works:

1st exposure (*Rejection*)	"I reject it because it conflicts with my preconceived ideas."
2nd exposure (*Resistance*)	"Well, I understand it. But I can't accept it."
3rd exposure (*Partial acceptance*)	"I agree. But I have reservations about its use."
4th exposure (*Full acceptance*)	"You know, that idea expresses the way I have been thinking."
5th exposure (*Partial assimilation*)	"I used that idea today. It's terrific."
6th exposure (*Full assimilation*)	"I gave the idea to a friend yesterday. In the truest sense of the words, the idea now belongs to me."

Affirmations are highly effective for Personality Development. Be patient. They work on the Displacement Principle. Do not look for a miracle. But instead, look for a method.

Sample Affirmations

Self-Respect
I respect myself. I am as good as anyone else. My potentials are limitless.

Memory
My memory is excellent. I can remember everything of importance to me. To make it work even better, I need only attach more importance to those experiences that I do want to remember.

Composure
I am in complete control of myself at all times. I am able to respect the arguments of others and accept challenges and disagreements calmly.

Relaxation
I am able to relax as completely as I wish at any time. I conserve my energy and direct it towards those goals that are meaningful to me.

Reading
I understand reading as a digestive process. I am an efficient reader. To be even more efficient, I need only vary my speed and method of reading according to my own personal needs.

Concentration
I have the ability to focus my undivided attention on any particular task at any time. I am able to isolate any single subject in my mind and concentrate deeply on it. I focus my attention on the problem at hand, oblivious to the world around me.

29

Knowledge: Means or an End

> "Those who have read and re-read the text of all the four Vedas, the Scriptures, and of the books on Law, but have failed to realise the Self, are just like a ladle moving in the cooking pan without relishing the taste of what is being cooked."
>
> CHANAKYA
> Ancient Indian statesman

You and I were taught to add the term 'great' after such famous names like Alexander and Napoleon. Most of us never thought about it, nor did we have an opportunity to ask the teacher what they were 'great' for. The teacher called them 'great' and they became great for us too. This directly has led to a situation, whereby, when some young man gives a speech on greatness today, he quotes an Alexander or a Napoleon Bonaparte.

My basic reference here is to ask myself what these two people were truly great for, and do I know the correct answer?

Today, after so many years, let me attempt an answer to myself.

Essentially, Alexander was a hard, ambitious person who wanted to conquer the entire world. He used all his talents and powers to gather and to train thousands of people, essentially for killing others, acquiring their wealth, and properties, and in the process becoming the Emperor of the whole world himself.

What did Alexander accomplish through all these? Did he conquer the world? (We do agree that he had many sterling qualities.) But, with all his actions, *what did he accomplish?* To me he could only succeed in killing thousands of innocent people, and, causing enormous pain and sufferings to his own people. He himself died a pauper. How sad!

Alexander is not remembered today for any worthwhile contributions he could make to his own country or to the humanity at large. Yes, he succeeded in killing so many innocent people. Is this the intended lesson for our young ones to be taught in our schools?

A similar and current example could be of Saddam Hussein of Iraq. Should we teach our children to grow up like Saddam Hussein and to learn to be like him?

It is often quoted that just before his death, Alexander instructed his people that when he died, both his hands must be left outside his coffin. He was, with such an action, confessing to the whole world that through all his so-called heroic deeds, he was unable to carry anything with him during his last journey.

It is my considered opinion, that his last action alone can attribute 'greatness' to Alexander. At least he realised something important a few moments before his impending death.

In his quest to conquer the world, Alexander had to turn back after his Indian experience. His own people were revolting against him.

What did Napoleon Bonaparte accomplish which can be taught to our children as great?

What did Idi Amin of Uganda accomplish?

What did Ayatollah Khomeini accomplish?

What did Saddam Hussein accomplish so far? An oil-rich nation which is ruled by him, is now reeling under poverty and untold miseries!

Knowledge: Means or an End

Compare these against the Japanese after the Second World War.

There is the comparable case of Emperor Ashoka of India. He too went about his kingly duties the way Alexander did. In the process, he noticed the suffering and losses that were caused to thousands of people after the Kalinga war. He saw the sorrows, the pain and the grief his actions had caused to the people. He was moved by the plight of the widows and the mothers who had lost their dear ones during the war.

Ashoka contemplated on this. He felt moved, sad and disturbed. This made him change. He gave up wars. He accepted Buddhism as his religion. And, he spent the rest of his life bringing welfare and prosperity to his people.

Emperor Ashoka is remembered only for the good he brought about for his nation after the Kalinga war. Today, the official insignia of India is the 'Ashoka Chakra' which also contains the motto "SATYAMEVA JAYATHE"—Truth Alone Shall Prevail. Do I as an Indian feel proud about Ashoka? Yes, but only for all those things he did after the Kalinga war.

We have talked about Mahatma Gandhi earlier. The term 'Mahatma', when translated, reads 'The Great Soul'. Thus, Gandhi the Great.

Does the greatness of Alexander, Napoleon or an Idi Amin rank in the same level as that of Ashoka, Gandhi, Martin Luther King Jr. or Nelson Mandela of South Africa?

While referring to great leaders, whom should we or our children quote?

Have we referred only to great political leaders so far? Is it fair? Why not refer to myself? Why not to yourself?

How shall I be considered as a great parent by my own children? By the number of beatings and scoldings I have given them?

How could I be considered as a great husband? By the cheating and the manipulating I have done on my wife to justify my own needs?

How shall I be considered as a good brother, or a neighbour, or teacher, or a grandfather?

How could I be considered as a great Manager or a Supervisor or an Artist or a Human Being?

KNOWING and KNOWLEDGE are two different things.

KNOWING comes from direct learning; from direct experience. It is a part of your extensional world.

The taste of the apple you ate, or the joy you felt while watching a dance, or the pain you endured when a friend cheated on you, or the skill you possess in tuning up an engine, are things you know. They are within you. They did not come to you through words or books.

KNOWLEDGE comes to you from the reports of others. It is a part of your verbal world.

All the history and the geography (and so many other topics) that you learned from books, is mere knowledge to you. When you directly experience some of the things stated there, they become a part of your KNOWING too.

We (You and I) must understand the role of KNOWLEDGE in helping us to become well-developed personalities.

Pursuit of knowledge for its own sake and as an end in itself, is often seen as an all-consuming goal of a modern, educated individual.

Every person wants to live happily. If knowledge alone could achieve this end, then all our scholars should be the happiest people. Are they?

Beware! KNOWLEDGE is not the end.

You can exist in two ways.

You can exist as a head-oriented person. You will succeed in the world. You will accumulate riches, prestige, and power. In politics, you will be a successful man. In the eyes of the world you will become the pinnacle to be aspired to. But in your inner world, you will fail completely, you will fail utterly. Because, the head-oriented person cannot enter the inner world. The head moves outwardly.

The heart opens inwards. It is an opening into yourself.

The man of the heart is a man of love. He does not bother himself with questions like where the universe originated from. He does not bother about who created it. He does not bother where it is leading to. In fact, without asking any unwanted questions, he starts living.

EXPERIENCE is a result of learning from everything that happens to us in our day-to-day living. Literacy or modern education, though it helps, is not essential for gaining EXPERIENCE.

Knowledge: Means or an End

Knowing, Knowledge and Experience are means to acquiring *WISDOM*. Knowledge which does not help in acquiring *WISDOM*, can be dangerous too.

All the things dished out to us by the mass media may increase our knowledge. But, when we consistently seek the truth, and in the process, acquire more WISDOM, we shall grow into happy individuals.

WISDOM is the goal; our goal. This is your purpose in developing your Personality further. My purpose is to assist you in your purpose.

May you be *Wise*.
May you be *Happy*.